Wo
El

D0818934

FIELD GUIDE

Edited by Paul Kennedy

Values and Identification

©2005 KP Books
Published by

kp books
An Imprint of F+W Publications

700 East State Street • Iola, WI 54990-0001
715-445-2214 • 888-457-2873
Our toll-free number to place an order or obtain
a free catalog is (800) 258-0929.

Library of Congress Catalog Number: 2004115356
ISBN: 0-89689-136-4

Designed by Kay Sanders
Edited by Paul Kennedy

Printed in United States of America

Elvis photographs provided by Bob Klein of Bob Klein
Photo Archives (www.TCBphotos.com). Special thanks to
Marc and Debra Zakarin of It's Only Rock n' Roll
(www.itsonlyrocknroll.com); and writer Chris Nickson.

Contents

The King knew how to shake it: 1967's "Jailhouse Rock."

Long Live the King

By Chris Nickson

Few entertainers are instantly recognized by one name. Throughout history there are no more than a handful. Liberace? Maybe, but he was more spectacle than anything else. Lassie? Godzilla? Sorry, but dogs and science fiction monsters don't count. Madonna and Cher? Sure. But even these divas of pop music and limited movie fame pale in comparison to the man who would be King – Elvis.

Even now, almost 30 years after his death, Elvis Presley casts a giant shadow, not only over music, but all of American culture. Without him, rock 'n' roll and all of pop music as we know it would not be the same. Without him, one could argue, America might well be a different place. His 1950s recordings established the basic language of rock 'n' roll; his explosive and sexual stage presence set standards for all performers who followed; and his movies made it possible for an entire world to see and hear him.

Elvis burst onto the music scene in the summer of 1954.

It's truly stunning to realize that Elvis has sold over a billion records all around the world. In America alone, he's garnered an incredible 149 gold or platinum discs (gold means half a million sales, platinum a million). Eighteen of his singles went to number one in the U.S. pop charts, as did 10 of his albums. No other American artist has managed to come close to his achievements.

Through it all, however, Elvis was far more than a singer. To the world, he came to typify America and the American dream.

Elvis Aaron Presley was born Jan. 8, 1935, in Tupelo, Mississippi, to Vernon and Gladys Presley. The family was poor and lived a hardscrabble life, moving around a little, but always returning to Tupelo.

Music became a consuming passion of Elvis' life. He performed on local radio, and by seventh grade he was taking his guitar to school every day, playing for the other kids at lunchtime. In 1948, the Presleys made a giant move to Memphis, trying to escape the poverty that had been grinding them down in Tupelo. Vernon found a job at United Paint, and the family settled into a public housing apartment in Lauderdale Courts.

At Humes High School Elvis was a quiet, shy student. At home he eagerly absorbed all the different music on the

Elvis received a guitar on his 12th birthday from his mother.

Memphis radio stations, the blues, country and gospel that filled the airwaves. By his junior year he'd started to develop the famous hairstyle that would become his trademark. The hair and the more distinctive clothes he began wearing marked him as different than his classmates. But he largely kept his musical talents hidden, astonishing his classmates when he played and sang at a school talent contest in his senior year.

Elvis first arrived at Sam Phillips' Memphis Recording Service in the summer of 1953 to record two songs as a gift for his mother. He kept returning, hungry and eager for a break, and Phillips eventually recommended him to guitarist Scotty Moore, who led a band named the Wranglers. Elvis, Moore and bassist Bill Black went into Memphis Recording Service on July 5, 1954. The session proved unproductive until, on a break, Elvis began fooling around on a blues song, Arthur Crudup's "That's All Right," and the others joined in. Suddenly the spark ignited, and Sam Phillips was there to fan it. It was something new, not country, not blues, not rhythm and blues, but a performance that welded all three styles into one. It was new and utterly different.

Three nights later disc jockey Dewey Phillips (no relation) played the song on his popular Memphis radio show, and the phone lines lit up. The Elvis explosion had begun.

Elvis' first No. 1 record was "Heartbreak Hotel" in 1956.

Soul, sideburns and sex appeal: The Elvis recipe for success.

Elvis graduated from L.C. Humes High School, Memphis.

That single – released on Phillips' Sun label - established Elvis throughout the South, as kids latched on to this new style of music, this rock 'n' roll that was so exciting. Before the end of the year Elvis was a regular on the "Louisiana Hayride" radio show, broadcast throughout the South. Show bookings flooded in.

Elvis' five Sun singles – "That's All Right Mama," "Blue Moon of Kentucky," "Good Rockin' Tonight," "Baby Let's Play House," and "Mystery Train" – remain core early rock classics. Some consider the five songs not only Elvis' best singles, but also the best rock 'n' roll ever recorded.

Through 1955 things moved so quickly that Elvis could barely keep pace, releasing more singles on Sun and touring nationally. When ex-carny Col. Tom Parker took over as his manager, he was on the cusp of becoming a major star. And once RCA bought Elvis' contract from a cash-strapped Sun, everything was in place to make Elvis Presley the first major star of the rock era.

But no one realized the magnitude of that stardom. How could they? By March 1956 Elvis had sold almost a million copies of "Heartbreak Hotel," his first number one record. He was playing sold-out, riotous concerts across the country, even giving his first Vegas performance. His records sold like hotcakes. He made his first movie and appeared on "The

Elvis (far right) on the Steve Allen Show with (from left) Andy Griffith, Imogene Coca and host Steve Allen.

Ed Sullivan Show," cropped from the waist down, so his gyrations wouldn't inflame teenage girls. Elvis the Pelvis had truly arrived.

Yet his success had barely started. The singles kept on coming, each one a huge hit. "Jailhouse Rock" cemented his popularity. He needed a retreat, and found it in the property of Graceland, the Memphis mansion he bought and remodeled. It was his sanctuary, and his fantasy, the family home he'd always wanted for his parents and himself. He could spend time there, alone or with his friends, and just relax in the brief moments when he wasn't touring, recording, or shooting a picture.

But just as it seemed that nothing could stop the momentum, something did – the United States government. In 1958 Elvis Presley was drafted. He could probably have arranged a way out of it, but he didn't even try. To him, it was part of being an American: there was no question of him not going. Cameras recorded the famous hair being cut. He was in the Army now. But before he could even complete basic training, tragedy struck: His beloved mother, Gladys, died.

Elvis was distraught. He had been particularly close to his mother, and he'd never completely recover from the loss.

After the funeral he was stationed in Germany. Some thought that would be the end of his career, that he'd be

Elvis made $50,000 to appear on The Ed Sullivan Show *in '56.*

forgotten during his two years away from the limelight. But he had spent plenty of time in the studio; recordings had been stockpiled. Instead of disappearing, his star rose even higher as he served his country.

While overseas, Elvis began dating 14 year-old Priscilla Beaulieu, the daughter of an Air Force officer. The

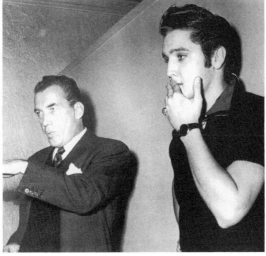

Elvis appeared three times on The Ed Sullivan Show.

relationship grew, and after Elvis returned to the States, she eventually followed him, living with Vernon Presley and his new wife, Dee, in Memphis. Although her relationship with Elvis was deep, they wouldn't marry until 1967.

Once his Army stint had ended, the focus of Elvis' career shifted. Instead of returning to the road and touring,

Elvis entered the US Army on March 24, 1958. He left active duty with the rank of sergeant on March 5, 1960.

he concentrated on films. The rock 'n' roll that had characterized his early sound was gone too, replaced by ballads and pop songs. This was the new Elvis, a little older, a little sleeker.

All around, music was changing. The British Invasion saw to that. But Elvis had influenced all those who followed him, including the Beatles. One of their biggest thrills when touring the U.S. was to meet him. His singles and albums continued to sell in enormous quantities, and his films were all guaranteed hits at the box office. Elvis still had the Midas touch

He spent his free time with Priscilla, with family, and with the group of old friends who became known as the Memphis Mafia. They were the buffer between him and the world. With them he could let his hair down, and be just plain old Elvis, instead of the superstar everyone expected.

Col. Parker continued to guide his career. And the fans remained faithful; indeed, they couldn't get enough of Elvis. The one thing they all wanted was to see him perform live again.

And Elvis himself was ready to return to the stage, to enjoy the communication with his fans, and the spontaneity of performance in front of an audience. In 1968 he did exactly that, taping the aptly named "68 Comeback Special" in front of an invited crowd. In black leather, on a small stage, he played a great show of old material. Aired on NBC in

Elvis met his future wife, Priscilla Beaulieu, 14, in Germany.

December 1968, it showed Elvis was still a vital artist, and an icon of rock 'n' roll.

It marked the beginning of a new phase in Elvis' career, the Elvis of Vegas and elaborate concert tours, a long way from the rough informality of his early appearances. He'd grown into a charismatic performer, backed by an outstanding band. He was back with a vengeance, proving his relevance with new material like "Suspicious Minds" and "In The Ghetto."

He might no longer have been the all-out rocker of the '50s, but along the way he'd grown in stature to become indefinable, an entertainer everyone wanted to see – and more especially, hear. The sequined jumpsuits, capes and scarves became his uniform, and audiences kept flocking to Las Vegas for his shows, consistently breaking attendance records, and he filled the halls whenever he ventured around the country.

He was, perhaps, at his happiest right then. His music had rarely sounded better, he was married, and the father of a little girl, Lisa Marie. A staggering 1.5 billion people saw his 1973 TV special, "Elvis: Aloha from Hawaii." He'd reached more peaks, both personally and professionally.

But slowly things would begin to crumble. He and Priscilla divorced, and his health started to deteriorate;

Elvis and Priscilla were married May 1, 1967, in Las Vegas.

periodically, shows and tours had to be canceled. Elvis became a more isolated, haunted figure, dividing his time between luxury penthouse suites in Vegas hotels and his beloved Graceland. His weight fluctuated wildly and he became dependent upon a variety of prescription drugs.

Yet he could still be stunning. "From Elvis Presley Boulevard, Memphis, Tennessee" went straight to the top of the country charts, and he supported it with a lengthy stint on the road that ran into 1977. Three concerts in June 1977 were taped by CBS for their "Elvis in Concert" special.

By then, however, it was apparent that Elvis wasn't in good shape. On June 26 he performed in Indianapolis. It would be his last show, although no one realized it at the time. Elvis died on August 16, 1977, at home in Graceland. The King was dead.

Or was he?

In death Elvis became greater than he had in life. People from all over the world flocked to his funeral in Memphis. In October his coffin was moved, along with that of his mother, to rest permanently at Graceland. Elvis had come home.

On the first anniversary of his death, thousands came to the house to pay their respects, and still do every August. Even now, streams of people arrive every day to visit Graceland, to see where Elvis lived, and the things he surrounded himself with.

The "68 Comeback Special" renewed interest in Elvis' career.

He remains a multi-million dollar business. Collections of Elvis songs still sell in the millions. He's been well served with expansive box sets that have delved deep into the archives to offer very full pictures of his music. Countless books have been written about him, covering every facet of his life in detail. Elvis has become an industry.

Some believe he never actually died at all, and just ran away from his life to start over. According to rumor and untold supermarket tabloid stories, he's been spotted working in a convenience store in Michigan, eating a pizza in London and many other places.

Even now, the world can't get enough of Elvis. Hundreds of Elvis impersonators exist; some of them make a good living by being the King. A remix of "A Little Less Conversation" (the first time the Presley Estate had sanctioned such a thing) was a European #1 in 2002. Twenty-five years after this death, Elvis was back on top of the charts.

Bigger than the life that bound him, Elvis has become a legend, the legend of rock 'n' roll, one that towers above all others. And for as long as people listen to music, and remain interested in America and its unique culture, that's what he'll remain. Others have come along and tried to dethrone, but no one's succeeded. Nor will they; this King rules forever!

Elvis recaptured his career in the late 1960s and early 1970s.

Elvis Field Guide

Elvis turned Las Vegas on its ear with dynamite shows in '75.

The face that launched a million teen-aged girl screams.

The King performing on the Steve Allen Show in 1956.

Nothing compared to the electricity of Elvis in concert.

Elvis and the Blue Moon Boys first performed in 1954.

Scotty Moore, lead guitarist of the Blue Moon Boys, and Elvis.

Scotty Moore (left) once served as Elvis' manager.

The Million Dollar Quarter: Jerry Lee Lewis, Carl Perkins, Johnny Cash and Elvis, Sun Records studio, Dec. 4, 1956.

Elvis and the Blue Moon Boys (Bill Black, Scotty Moore and D.J. Fontana) relax outside the Frontier in Las Vegas, 1956.

Elvis rubbed fans the right way. And they did the same for him.

Elvis with a fan at a local roller rink early in his career.

Elvis shares a moment with some of his Memphis fans.

The album "Elvis Presley" is released in 1956. It reaches No. 1.

Elvis signed his first movie contract with Paramount in 1956.

The first national story on Elvis ran in Life, April 30, 1956.

Elvis' first job was with Crown Electric driving a delivery truck.

Elvis' only commercial was for Southern Made Doughnuts.

Young people embraced Elvis right away, especially female fans.

Although sexy, Elvis was quite innocent early in his career.

By 1956, even Elvis was reading about Elvis.

Elvis always danced to the beat of a different drummer.

Elvis outside Graceland, which he bought in March 1957.

Elvis moved into the 23-room Graceland mansion in June 1957.

When Elvis met Liberace in Las Vegas in 1956 he asked for an autograph for his mother, Gladys. Liberace happily obliged.

Elvis first met Bill Haley in October 1955. Elvis played on the same bill with Haley at the height of his "Rock Around the Clock" fame. Elvis and Haley became fast friends.

Elvis met Sammy Davis, Jr., on the movie set of "Loving You."

Elvis first appeared on the Milton Berle Show in April 1956.

Elvis at home posing in his famous gold suit.

Elvis Presley Day is declared Sept. 9, 1956, in Tupelo, Miss.

Colonel Tom Parker became Elvis' manager in August of 1955.

A female fan lends Elvis a hand. And he autographs it.

Ed Sullivan once called Elvis "a decent, fine boy."

Bootleg Elvis recordings reached the Soviet Union in 1957.

Elvis performed in Hawaii for the first time in November, 1957.

Elvis first performed in Canada in April of 1957.

Elvis relaxing poolside at the Frontier in Las Vegas, 1956.

Las Vegas would become the King's home-away-from-home.

Elvis captured backstage prior to the Steve Allen Show, 1956.

Elvis rehearsing on stage for The Ed Sullivan show.

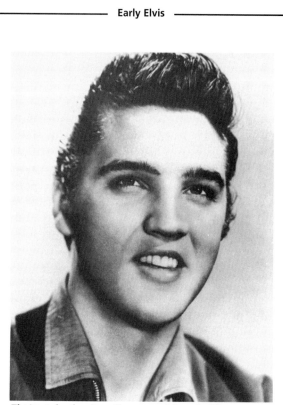

Elvis' twin brother, Jesse Garon, was delivered stillborn.

Elvis loved cars and was famous for giving them as presents.

Elvis with The Jordanaires on The Ed Sullivan Show.

Jana Lund gave Elvis his first screen kiss in "Loving You."

*Elvis with special friend Judy Spreckels and cousin Gene Smith.
Spreckels is said to have been like a sister to Elvis.*

Elvis and Spreckels met in Vegas and became lifetime friends.

Elvis' image was used on a U.S. postage stamp released in 1993.

There are an estimated 625 active Elvis fan clubs worldwide.

A peanut butter and banana sandwich was an Elvis favorite.

Elvis had 149 songs appear on Billboard's Hot 100 charts.

Elvis and Priscilla are married May 1, 1967, in Las Vegas.

The couple had a second reception at Graceland on May 29.

Elvis had 18 songs that went to No. 1 on the Billboard charts.

Elvis was inducted into the Rock 'n' Roll Hall of Fame in 1986.

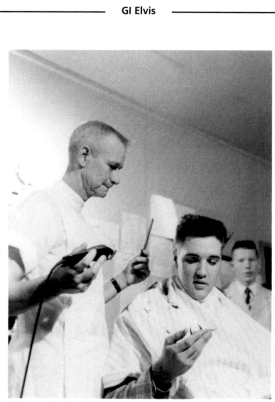

Elvis gets his famous GI haircut at Fort Chaffee, Arkansas.

Elvis considered it an honor to serve his country in the Army.

Elvis had six months of basic training at Fort Hood, Texas.

Elvis had no problem staying close to his fans, even in the Army.

Elvis signed plenty of autographs in his two-year military stint.

The movie "King Creole" opened in 1958 to rave reviews.

Elvis' mother became ill in August 1958. She died Aug. 14.

Many believed Elvis never recovered from his mother's death.

In Germany, Elvis was stationed in Friedberg for 18 months.

Elvis lived off base with his father while stationed in Germany.

Elvis' serial number was 53310761. To fans he was still No. 1.

Elvis belonged to a tank battalion while serving his country.

The fans in Europe were as enthusiastic as those in the States.

Elvis was promoted to sergeant Jan. 20, 1960.

Elvis left Germany on March 1, 1960, arriving in New Jersey.

Huge crowds of adoring fans greeted Elvis' return home.

Elvis did not perform publicly while stationed in Germany.

Despite fears, Elvis' music remained popular while in the Army.

Private Presley learned firsthand why they call it boot camp.

Music was a big part of apartment life for Elvis in Germany.

Elvis and his father, Vernon, enjoy some time together.

Elvis was officially discharged from active duty March 5, 1960.

Elvis served his country like any other GI, with few privileges.

In the end, the time in the Army made Elvis an even bigger star.

Elvis struck a chord with fans in 1961's "Blue Hawaii."

Elvis Goes Hollywood

By Chris Nickson

There are two opposing schools of thought about Elvis and his movies. For many fans, they were wonderful, offering more chances to see him – and in greater close-up – than if he'd been touring. To others, Elvis' rock 'n' roll career died when he went Hollywood.

Whichever side of the fence you're on, the simple fact is that the 31 movies Elvis made were all box office successes, and took him to a level of stardom far beyond music. In the mid 1950s, rock was still seen as something dangerous, something that could subvert a nation's youth; movies, on the other hand, were all-American entertainment.

It was Col. Tom Parker's idea to put Elvis into films. To him, rock was simply a fad that could end at any time. The movies seemed to offer longevity, if Elvis could establish himself in Hollywood. And that proved far easier than expected. "Love Me Tender" became an immediate hit in 1956, then the machine cranked into action, following it with "Loving You," and the first of Elvis's great films, "Jailhouse Rock." With some classic staging and great songs (the title cut and "(You're So Square) Baby I Don't Care"), it stood as one of the best American films of a fertile decade.

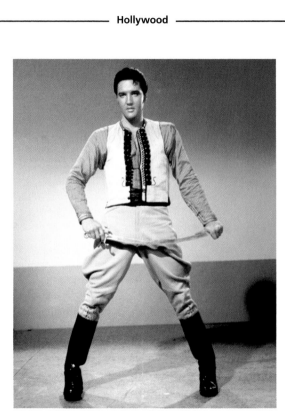

Elvis in MGM's "Harum Scarum" from 1965.

Naturally, Elvis films were conceived as musicals, spawning hit singles, EPs and soundtrack albums, all of which were snapped up by fans in great quantities (and would be for as long as he made movies). In 1958, before the momentum of the Elvis film industry could really reach full speed, he was drafted into the armed service. There was time to crank out "Kid Creole" before he left, but then there was a two-year gap – and plenty of chewed fingernails, as executives wondered if his popularity would last while he was out of the public eye.

They needn't have worried. Just like rock 'n' roll, the stardom of Elvis Presley wasn't about to fade away.

The movie "GI Blues" was a natural comeback once Elvis returned from the service, a way to capitalize on his experiences, and his heroic status for serving his country rather than using influence to avoid the draft. It ushered in the era when Elvis focused solely on his film and recording careers. He didn't tour, he didn't even play concerts, and wouldn't until his famed 1968 comeback. If you wanted to see Elvis – and so many did – the silver screen was the only option.

But there was certainly no lack of opportunity to catch him there. Two or three films a year rapidly became the norm. The films were churned out on what seemed to be a

Donna Douglas and Elvis in 1966's "Frankie and Johnny."

production line. They were serviceable vehicles for Elvis and his songs, entertainments that never pretended to be more than happy fluff. Yet a few did tower above the crowd, like "Kid Galahad" and "Viva Las Vegas," where the scripts and cast allowed Elvis to truly shine.

From his screen test on, Elvis had shown a natural aptitude for acting. He cut a charismatic figure on screen, and he inhabited his characters, even the flimsy ones. While even his most ardent fan couldn't call all his films masterpieces, Elvis never turned in a bad performance.

It didn't hurt the movies that Elvis' love interests in the movies included such leading ladies as Juliet Prowse, Tuesday Weld, Ann-Margaret, Mary Tyler Moore, and Ursula Andress. Inevitably there was talk of his involvement with a few of them, such as Debra Paget, who worked with him on "Love Me Tender" and who remained a close friend.

Yet there was also an auspicious list of male talent in Elvis' films. Walter Matthau, Dean Jagger, Charles Bronson, Jackie Coogan, Michael Ansara, Harry Morgan, Burgess Meredith and Bill Bixby were just a few of the well-known names who popped up in the credits.

So why did Elvis finally stop making movies? They'd been a reliable vehicle for him for years, a way to be seen by literally millions all around the globe. Quite simply, they'd

Elvis on the set for the 1960 release "Flaming Star."

stopped being a challenge. He'd conquered Hollywood, at least as far as he was able. Elvis movies were about fun, a little romance, and some songs, and the studios were more than content to keep them that way. They were almost like a license to print money, and there was no incentive to tamper with the formula. So Elvis never had the chance to test himself with darker, more dramatic material. And, as he grew older, there was more of a desire to return to music, his first love.

His life had changed: Elvis was now married, and the father of Lisa Marie. Hollywood, and the life that went with it, had been great, but it wasn't a place for a family and a baby. It was time to go home to Memphis, to make Graceland into a real home once more.

His movies continued appearing until 1969, because of existing contracts (and one of the last was one of his best, "Charro!"). But from that point Elvis never set foot on a movie soundstage again, although he made several television specials. It was as if an era had ended, and suddenly he'd forgotten it ever existed and moved on to the next chapter in his life.

The films Elvis made truly cemented his popularity. Before his screen appearances the only chances to see him had been on television. Overseas fans hadn't even enjoyed

Ann-Margaret and Elvis sizzled in 1964's "Viva Las Vegas."

that opportunity. To have him up close and larger than life was every fan's dream come true. Then to also have him sing, well, for the global market as it was in those days, film was the perfect device. Movies helped turn Elvis into the world's first superstar, recognized everywhere. With the advent of video, Elvis' films found a new, devoted audience, although not all his work has yet been issued on DVD.

Love them or hate them, the films Elvis made transformed him.

Elvis in the 1966 Western "Charro."

The Elvis Movies

1. "Love Me Tender" (1956)

2. "Loving You" (1957)

3. "Jailhouse Rock" (1957)

4. "King Creole" (1958)

5. "GI Blues" (1960)

6. "Flaming Star" (1960)

7. "Wild in the Country" (1961)

8. "Blue Hawaii" (1961)

9. "Follow That Dream" (1962)

10. "Kid Galahad" (1962)

11. "Girls! Girls! Girls!" (1962)

12. "It Happened at the World's Fair" (1963)

13. "Fun in Acapulco" (1963)

14. "Kissin' Cousins" (1964)

15. "Viva Las Vegas" (1964)

The Elvis Movies

16. "Roustabout" (1964)

17. "Girl Happy" (1965)

18. "Tickle Me" (1965)

19. "Harum Scarum" (1965)

20. "Frankie and Johnny" (1966)

21. "Paradise, Hawaiian Style" (1966)

22. "Spinout" (1966)

23. "Easy Come, Easy Go" (1967)

24. "Double Trouble" (1967)

25. "Clambake" (1967)

26. "Stay Away, Joe" (1968)

27. "Speedway" (1968)

28. "Live a Little, Love a Little" (1968)

29. "Charro!" (1969)

30. "The Trouble with Girls" (1969)

31. "Change of Habit" (1969)

Elvis and Debra Paget in 1956's "Love Me Tender."

Richard Egan, not Elvis, got top billing in "Love Me Tender."

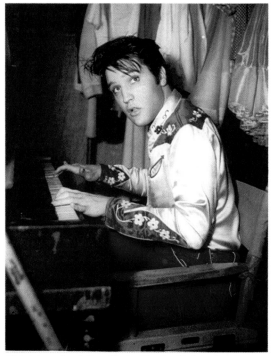

Elvis takes a break from filming "Loving You" to play piano.

Dolores Hart played Elvis' love interest in 1957's "Loving You."

Elvis goes to the Big House in 1957's "Jailhouse Rock."

Elvis had the whole cell block dancing to the "Jailhouse Rock."

Elvis and Carolyn Jones cast a large shadow in "King Creole."

Juliet Prowse and Elvis heat up the screen in 1960's "GI Blues."

"GI Blues" was hardly a stretch for the service-returning Elvis.

Barbara Eden and Elvis in 1960's "Flaming Star."

Hope Lange snuggles up with Elvis in "Wild in the Country."

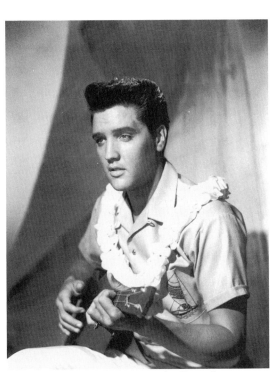

Elvis stars as Chad Gates in 1961's "Blue Hawaii."

Trainer Charles Bronson handles Elvis in 1962's "Kid Galahad."

Elvis as boat captain Ross Carpenter in "Girls, Girls, Girls."

Elvis sang the smash "Return to Sender" in "Girls, Girls, Girls."

Elvis in 1963's "It Happened at the World's Fair."

Elvis plays a flawed pilot in "It Happened at the World's Fair."

Elvis plays a former trapeze artist in 1963's "Fun in Acapulco."

Elvis played two roles in the forgettable "Kissin' Cousins."

A publicity shot from one of Elvis' best films, "Viva Las Vegas."

Elvis takes Barbara Stanwyck for a ride in "Roustabout."

Elvis plays carny Charlie Rogers in 1964's "Roustabout."

A good soundtrack saved the day in 1965's "Girl Happy."

Elvis Field Guide

Elvis plays Lonnie Beal in 1965's "Tickle Me."

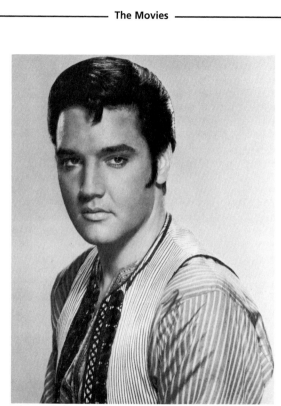

Elvis is a kidnapped matinee idol in 1965's "Harum Scarum."

Elvis on the set of 1966's "Frankie and Johnny."

Elvis enjoys the natural beauty in "Paradise, Hawaiian Style."

Elvis plays a singing race car driver in 1966's "Spinout."

Elvis with Pat Priest in 1967's "Easy Come, Easy Go."

Elvis and Annette Day in 1967's "Double Trouble."

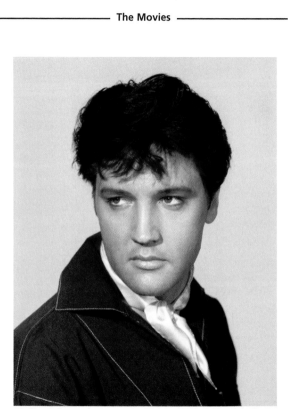

Shelley Fabares plays opposite Elvis in 1967's "Clambake."

Elvis plays a Navajo bull rider in 1968's "Stay Away, Joe."

Elvis starred in 31 movies, often doing as many as three a year.

In "Stay Away, Joe," Elvis actually had to sing to an under-performing bull named Dominick. It is easy to see why Elvis soon lost interest in making movies.

Elvis and Nancy Sinatra heat up the screen in "Speedway."

Elvis plays a photographer in "Live a Little, Love a Little."

Elvis is a framed gunslinger in 1968's "Charro."

Elvis Field Guide

Elvis as Walter Hale in 1969's "Trouble With Girls."

Elvis in his final feature film, 1969's "Change of Habit."

Elvis and Colonel Parker on the set of "Change of Habit."

The 1968 television comeback special was simply called "Elvis."

Powerful and passionate, Elvis wowed millions in his comeback.

Elvis had not performed in front of an audience for seven years.

NBC's "Elvis" showcased a 33-year-old star at his best.

"Elvis" was broadcast Dec. 3, 1968. The soundtrack hit No. 8.

Rock writer John Landau called the performance "magical."

The 1968 special motivated Elvis to return to live performances.

Fans once again swarmed the King for his autograph.

Elvis, smiling in Houston, was at the top of his game in 1970.

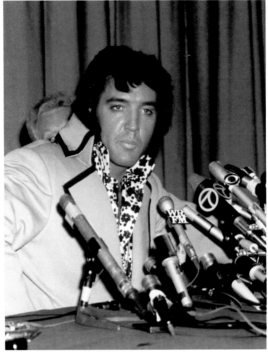

Elvis at a press conference at the Hilton in New York.

Elvis won a Grammy for 1972's album "He Touched Me."

Despite a career rebirth, Elvis and Priscilla separate in 1972.

Elvis on stage with the Supremes.

John Lennon and Bob Dylan saw Elvis perform in New York.

Elvis glowed in his 1972 concert in Madison Square Garden.

On the 1972 tour, Elvis broke concert attendance records.

Elvis scored a hit in 1972 with "Burning Love."

The King in "Elvis: Aloha from Hawaii" concert in 1973.

The Aloha concert attracts 51 percent of the U.S. TV audience.

Worldwide, more than 1 billion people watch the Aloha concert.

The Aloha concert proved to be the pinnacle of Elvis' career.

The Aloha soundtrack spent 52 weeks on Billboard's charts.

Elvis strutted in his famous "peacock" jumpsuit in 1974.

Elvis with the great James Burton during a 1974 concert.

Elvis battled health problems while touring regularly in 1974.

Elvis Field Guide

Elvis renovated a Convair 880 jet and named it the Lisa Marie.

Elvis was dogged by health problems throughout 1975.

Elvis Field Guide

A young fan showed her appreciation for the King.

Elvis has sold more than 1 billion records worldwide.

Elvis won a third Grammy for "How Great Thou Art" in 1975.

Elvis at the large iron gates of Graceland, his Memphis home.

Home is Where The Heart Is

By Chris Nickson

During his life, Graceland, Elvis Presley's 14-acre Memphis estate, was a symbol of his success. From the musical notes on the massive iron gates to the trophy building housing his enormous collection of gold and platinum records, Graceland was an extraordinary home for the world's biggest star.

Since his death, however, Graceland has taken on even more significance. It has become a vital piece of Elvis mythology. Graceland, featuring year-round tours, is the closest fans can come to knowing the man himself, seeing how he lived and even where he is buried.

With its impressive Colonial front and huge oak doors, it was the perfect residence for a superstar (although it wasn't the first house Elvis bought; that was on Audubon Avenue). It was, he said, "the residence of the heart," a place Elvis associated with his mother, and "all of this love that still remains within its walls. It's an enduring way of life for me."

More than anywhere else on earth, it was the center of his life. On the acres behind the famous music gate was where he felt safe and secure, where he entertained the

Graceland proved to be the retreat Elvis desperately needed.

friends who made up the Memphis Mafia. It was where he and his wife, Priscilla, were happy. It was where he was free from the pressures of stardom and able to enjoy its pleasures.

At its core, Graceland is an eminently Southern house, with the grandeur of a plantation, a Tara, moved inside the city. It was everything Elvis could aspire to, a far cry from the shotgun houses and housing projects where he had grown up. With it, he could give his parents, especially his mother Gladys, the luxury she'd been forced to live without for so long. To Elvis, Graceland was the American dream. It was a symbol of success beyond anything he could have dreamed, a place for his cars, his wife, his family, his life. And Graceland became a symbol of Elvis, of his fame, of the man, of the way he lived – and died.

Thousands make the pilgrimage to see the house every year, and have done so since it opened in 1982. Each August, Elvis fans of all ages from around the world come to gather in Memphis for Elvis Week – a commemoration of the music, magic and memories associated with the legacy of Elvis Presley. Other regular celebrations are held at Christmas (Elvis' favorite holiday) and in January to commemorate the King's birthday.

Guests on the 60 to 90-minute tour of Graceland take pleasure in a specially produced audio guide featuring the

The music room is part of the Graceland tour, which features an audio guide with the voices of Elvis and daughter Lisa Marie.

voices of Elvis and his daughter, Lisa Marie. But the visitors can only get part of the picture. Travel there and you can see the living room, music room, kitchen, television room, dining room, pool room, the famous "jungle" den (which looks as if it had been transported wholesale from Africa), and the bedroom where Elvis' parents slept. Away from the main house, you see the racquetball building and Elvis' original office. And finally, of course, there's the Meditation Garden, where Elvis and his family are buried, a place of quiet communion.

The long living room, with its massive sofa and glittering fireplace, is a showpiece. Beyond it, framed by gorgeous stained glass windows, lies the music room, a much simpler affair, dominated by a grand piano, and a small TV (Elvis, after all, loved television) up against the window.

The main hallway, dominated by a portrait of Elvis, leads past the stairs to a dining room of regal proportions and pomp, a place for a king to dine. These public rooms are kept as they were during Elvis' lifetime.

To find the heart of the man, though, you need to look a little deeper, and find the small shooting range he kept by the kitchen, where he and the guys would aim at targets. Or locate the area that was the original patio by the outdoor pool. In the late 1960s Elvis had it made into a room, 40 feet

A stage costume displayed in the Graceland Trophy building.

long, to house his slot car track. Eventually it became the trophy room, with twenty more feet added, and filled with his gold and platinum discs, certificates and medals.

Upstairs, however, remains private. There, if you can ever sneak away from the tour, is the King's bedroom. His bed, a nine-by-nine, double king size with a black headboard, immediately catches the eye. A crimson carpet covers the floor. The walls are covered in padded, tufted black suede. This was the private space, the inner sanctum, and Elvis' ultimate refuge from the world.

There's more to Graceland than the house itself. You can also visit the automobile museum, with Elvis' car collection on display, everything from the famous '55 pink Cadillac to the MG he drove in "Blue Hawaii" to his '73 Stutz Blackhawk and his Harleys. Ultimate (and unmarried) Elvis fans can even tie the knot at the Chapel in the Woods, nestled handily right next to Graceland.

Wherever you go in Graceland, though, there's one place to return to, the peaceful Meditation Garden. Yes, it's a cemetery, but more than that it's a place of peace and communion, with small, beautiful murals like stained glass windows painted on the walls. It's a place to think, to rest, a place for eternity. It's Elvis surrounded by the people and the place he loved above all others.

The King's grave is found in the Meditation Garden.

There, finally, you can find the soul of Elvis, and of Graceland. There's a soothing gentility about it, there in the middle of the grounds. To spend a few minutes there is to feel close to Elvis, to understand him, and to go away with a warm heart, back down the driveway and out of the music gate.

It's a visit every Elvis fan should make at some point. If you want to understand the King, to take a peek at what made him tick, it's all here.

Elvis will live on in people's hearts. Not only the fans that saw him perform, but new generations who discover him on disc, video, and in movies. And as long as the spirit of Elvis remains, Graceland will still attract a loyal, loving crowd.

For Graceland tour information call
(800) 238-2000.

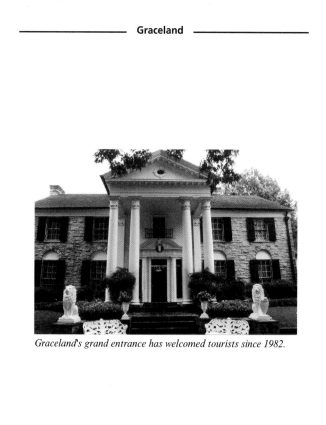

Graceland's grand entrance has welcomed tourists since 1982.

This is the last piano played by Elvis before his death in 1977.

The famous "Eagle" jumpsuit Elvis wore on stage.

Lavish and electric, Elvis' stage attire sparkled like the King.

Fans enjoy looking at the multitude of awards and honors Elvis earned throughout his legendary career.

The three Grammy Awards Elvis earned, all for Gospel music.

The "Lisa Marie" was named after Elvis' daughter. He referred to the jet as "The Pride of Elvis Presley Airways."

The Meditation Garden includes the Presley family graves.

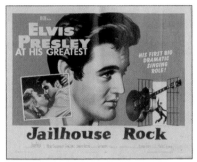

Elvis Presley "Jailhouse Rock" half-sheet movie poster. Poster from 1957 movie in VG-plus condition, $400.

Elvis Presley "Wild In The Country" half-sheet movie poster. Poster from 1961 movie in VG condition, $200.

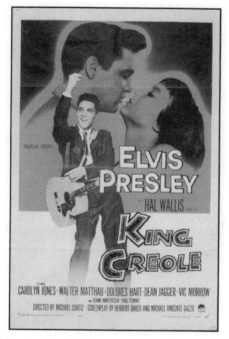

Elvis Presley "King Creole" one-sheet poster. From the 1958 movie featuring Elvis and Carolyn Jones, $200.

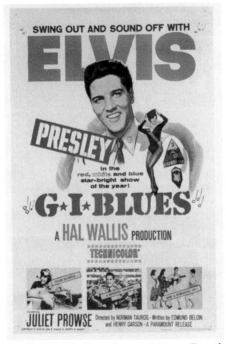

Elvis Presley "G.I. Blues" one-sheet movie poster: From the 1960 movie with Julie Prowse, EX condition, $400.

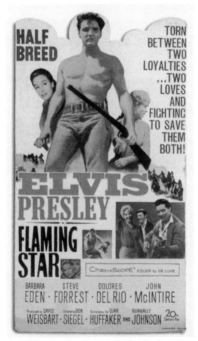

*Elvis Presley "Flaming Star" movie lobby display: From the
1960 movie, super rare, 32 x 58", corrugated display, $500.*

Elvis Presley "Blue Hawaii" cardboard lobby display: From the 1961 movie, extremely rare, 37" x 80", heavy cardboard, $1,200.

Elvis Presley Christmas Album Red Vinyl LP: The only red copy ever pressed of Elvis' first Christmas album (RCA LOC-1035), 1957, Mono. Unique Elvis collectible, includes original cover, **$23,500***.*

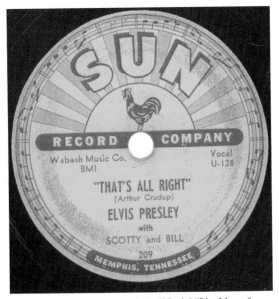

Elvis Presley's first Sun single, "That's All Right"/"Blue Moon of Kentucky." While Presley's original Sun 45s can sell for thousands of dollars, his five Sun 78s can command high prices as well.

$1,500, VG condition

What To Look For

The toughest task for an Elvis collector is to find his five Sun 45s (they are also available on 78s). Reproductions abound on these titles, and some of the reproductions actually use original out-of-stock Sun labels.

Any Sun Elvis recording pressed on colored or swirled vinyl is a reproduction; the originals were pressed only in black. There were never any "picture sleeves" for Elvis Sun recordings, either. And Sun never made any four-song EPs of Elvis' songs, so any that you find are phonies.

Of Presley's five Sun releases, legitimate copies of his first four releases have "push marks"—three circles pressed into the label itself. Not all the originals have push marks, but because the collectible value of a Sun 45 is extremely high, and since so many counterfeit and reproduced Sun 45s exist because of this, collectors look for the "push marks" to confirm a true Memphis pressing.

Presley's fifth Sun release, "Mystery Train"/"I Forgot to Remember to Forget" (Sun 223) does not contain push marks on the label. If the record has a triangle in the dead wax, the record was pressed by Monarch Record Pressing in Los Angeles. Even before his signing with RCA Victor, Elvis was already an established country music star from these Sun

If you look carefully on this Sun 45 label, you can see the circular "push mark" indentations, especially near the letters "TUC" in "Kentucky," and just to the right of the "Peer BMI" at 9 o'clock.

$6,000, NM condition

recordings, with "I Forgot To Remember To Forget" hitting #1 on the *Billboard* country charts.

During Presley's RCA tenure, the record company pressed millions of copies of his 45s and LPs. Within this, it is important to know not only the variations in label design throughout Elvis' recording career, but also when RCA changed their label patterns so that a collector can determine an original from a repressing.

Even though the front of an Elvis Presley album may contain the traditional RCA logos and trademarks of the 1950s, oftentimes the company would continue to press an old-style jacket with old-style logos, while inserting a new recording inside.

Web Pages

Elvis Presley's official page: *http://www.elvis. com*

Usenet newsgroups: *alt.fan.elvis-presley, alt.elvis.king*

How to Use This Record Guide

This section of the book is divided into three parts:

- Singles
- 7-inch extended play singles
- Albums

The singles are listed in alphabetical order by the title of the bigger hit side. In some cases where different editions of the same record declared a different A-side than the bigger hit, they are cross-referenced. The EPs and albums are listed alphabetically by the title.

Under each title we have listed the label and number and all the known variations, pretty much in the order they were available. Spelled out in detail is how to distinguish the different versions.

Finally, we list a range of values for copies in top-notch collectible condition. We have defined this as Very Good Plus at worst to Near Mint at best.

The prices are meant to be averages rather than maximums, although in some cases, they may be maximums. Some trusted dealers can, and will, sell items for more than the prices listed. They aren't trying to rip you off – you are also buying some of the trust and reputation that comes from dealing with them. Also, if you plan to sell your Elvis material, remember that if you are selling to a dealer, you will get a fraction of the quoted prices.

Elvis Presley
45 RPM Singles

Ain't That Loving You Baby/Ask Me

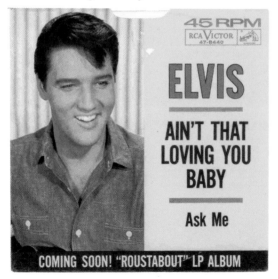

❑ RCA Victor 47-8440, black label, dog on top, 1964.. **5.00 - 10.00**

❑ RCA Victor 47-8440, white label promo, "Not for Sale"
on label, 1964...**30.00 - 60.00**

❑ RCA Victor 47-8440, picture sleeve, "Coming Soon 'Roustabout'
LP Album " on sleeve, 1964...........................**12.50 - 25.00**

❑ RCA Victor 47-8440, picture sleeve, "Ask For 'Roustabout' LP
Album" on sleeve, 1964................................**12.50 - 25.00**

❑ RCA Victor 447-0649, black label, dog on left, 1965 **5.00 - 10.00**

❑ RCA Victor 447-0649, red label, 1970..................**4.00 - 8.00**

❑ RCA 447-0649, black label, dog near top, no "Victor"
on label, 1977...**2.00 - 4.00**

❑ RCA Victor 47-8440, black label, dog on top, red vinyl, "DRE
13231" in trail-off wax, from box "Elvis Hit Singles Collection,
Volume 2," 2002...**2.00 - 4.00**

❑ RCA Victor 47-8440, picture sleeve, "Ask For 'Roustabout' LP
Album" on sleeve, "This is a replica of the original packaging"
on rear at bottom right, 2002.........................**2.00 - 4.00**

All Shook Up/That's When Your Heartaches Begin

❏ RCA Victor 47-6870, East Coast pressing with horizontal line on label, 1957..**15.00 - 30.00**

❏ RCA Victor 47-6870, Midwest or West Coast pressing with no horizontal line on label, 1957......................**15.00 - 30.00**

❑ RCA Victor 47-6870, picture sleeve, 1957 ....**45.00 - 90.00**

❑ RCA Victor 447-0618, black label, dog on top, 1959 **7.50 - 15.00**

❑ RCA Victor 447-0618, white label promo, "Not for Sale" on label,
  1964..**50.00 - 100.00**

❑ RCA Victor 447-0618, picture sleeve usually found with promo
  copies, 1964...**100.00 - 200.00**

❑ RCA Victor 447-0618, black label, dog on left, 1965 **5.00 - 10.00**

❑ RCA Victor 447-0618, orange label, 1969 ....**12.50 - 25.00**

❑ RCA Victor 447-0618, red label, 1970................**4.00 - 8.00**

❑ RCA 447-0618, black label, dog near top, no "Victor"
  on label, 1977.......................................**2.00 - 4.00**

❑ RCA PB-11106, from boxes "15 Golden Records, 30 Golden Hits"
  and "20 Golden Hits in Full Color Sleeves," 1977....**2.00 - 4.00**

❑ RCA PB-11106, picture sleeve, 1977.....................**2.00 - 4.00**

❑ RCA Victor 47-6870, black label, dog on top, red vinyl,
  "DRE1 3038" in trail-off wax, from box "Elvis #1 Hit
  Singles Collection," 2001................................**2.00 - 4.00**

❑ RCA Victor 47-6870, picture sleeve, "This is a replica of the
  original packaging" on rear at bottom, 2001 ....**2.00 - 4.00**

Always on My Mind (same on both sides)

❑ RCA JK-14090, purple vinyl promo, "Not for Sale"
  on label, 1985..**10.00 - 20.00**

Always on My Mind/My Boy

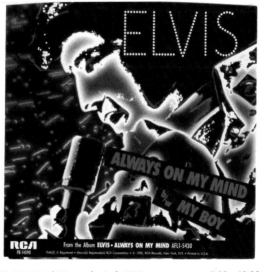

❑ RCA PB-14090, purple vinyl, 1985.....................**5.00 - 10.00**

❑ RCA PB-14090, picture sleeve, 1985....................**5.00 - 10.00**

**An American Trilogy/
The First Time Ever I Saw Your Face**

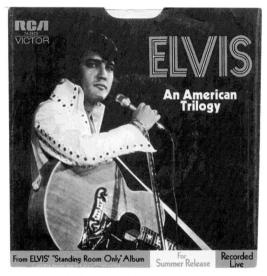

- ❑ RCA Victor 74-0672, orange label, 1972.............**10.00 - 20.00**
- ❑ RCA Victor 74-0672, yellow label promo, "Not for Sale"
  on label, 1972...**12.50 - 25.00**
- ❑ RCA Victor 74-0672, picture sleeve, 1972............**20.00 - 40.00**

An American Trilogy/
Until It's Time for You to Go

❑ RCA Victor 447-0685, red label, 1973...................**4.00 - 8.00**

❑ RCA 447-0685, black label, dog near top, 1977........**2.00 - 4.00**

❑ Collectables 80002, gray marbled vinyl, 1997..........**2.00 - 4.00**

Are You Lonesome Tonight/
Can't Help Falling in Love

❑ RCA PB-13895, from box "Elvis' Greatest Hits, Golden Singles,
   Volume 2"; gold vinyl, 1984..............................**2.00 - 4.00**

❑ RCA PB-13895, picture sleeve, 1984.....................**2.00 - 4.00**

Are You Lonesome To-Night?/I Gotta Know

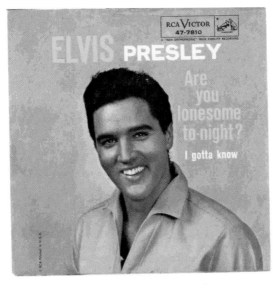

❑ RCA Victor 47-7810, black label, dog on top, 1960
....**10.00 - 20.00**

❑ RCA Victor 47-7810, picture sleeve, 1960 ....**30.00 - 60.00**

❑ RCA Victor 61-7810, "Living Stereo" on label,
   large hole, plays at 45 rpm, 1960 .... **300.00 - 600.00**

❑ RCA Victor 447-0629, black label, dog on top, 1962 **7.50 - 15.00**

❑ RCA Victor 447-0629, black label, dog on left, 1965 **5.00 - 10.00**

❑ RCA Victor 447-0629, orange label, 1969 .... **12.50 - 25.00**

❑ RCA Victor 447-0629, red label, 1970 .... **4.00 - 8.00**

❑ RCA 447-0629, black label, dog near top, no "Victor"
   on label, 1977 .... **2.00 - 4.00**

❑ RCA PB-11104, from boxes "15 Golden Records,
   30 Golden Hits" and "20 Golden Hits
   in Full Color Sleeves," 1977 .... **2.00 - 4.00**

❑ RCA PB-11104, picture sleeve, 1977 .... **2.00 - 4.00**

❑ RCA Victor 47-7810, black label, dog on top,
   red vinyl, "DRE1 3046" in trail-off wax, from box
   "Elvis #1 Hit Singles Collection," 2001 .... **2.00 - 4.00**

❑ RCA Victor 47-7810, picture sleeve, "This is a replica of the
   original packaging" on rear along left edge, 2001 .. **2.00 - 4.00**

Are You Sincere/Solitaire

❏ RCA JB-11533, yellow label, dog near top, promo, "Not for Sale" on label, 1979 .... **5.00 - 10.00**

❏ RCA PB-11533, black label, dog near top, 1979 .... **2.50 - 5.00**

❏ RCA PB-11533, picture sleeve, 1979 .... **5.00 - 10.00**

Ask Me/The Girl of My Best Friend

❑ Collectables COL-4738, 1997 .... **1.00 - 3.00**

Baby Let's Play House/Hound Dog

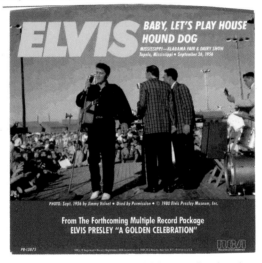

❑ RCA JB-13875, gold vinyl, custom label, promo, "Not for Sale" on label, 1984 .... **100.00 - 200.00**

❑ RCA PB-13875, gold vinyl, custom label, 1984 ...... **20.00 - 40.00**

❑ RCA PB-13875, picture sleeve, 1984 .... **20.00 - 40.00**

Baby Let's Play House/I'm Left, You're Right, She's Gone

Other than the 2001 sleeve listed, "picture sleeves" of Sun 217 and RCA Victor 47-6383 are bootlegs.

❑ Sun 217, 1955 (beware of counterfeits)...............**2,000 – 3,000**

❑ RCA Victor 47-6383, East Coast pressing with horizontal line on
   label, 1955 ....**30.00 - 60.00**

❑ RCA Victor 47-6383, Midwest or West Coast pressing with no
   horizontal line on label, 1955 ....**30.00 - 60.00**

❑ RCA Victor 447-0604, black label, dog on top, 1959 **7.50 - 15.00**

❑ RCA Victor 447-0604, black label, dog on left, 1965 **5.00 - 10.00**

❑ RCA Victor 447-0604, red label, 1970 ....**4.00 - 8.00**

❑ RCA 447-0604, black label, dog near top, no "Victor"
   on label, 1977 ....**2.00 - 4.00**

❑ Collectables COL-4502, black vinyl, 1986 ....**1.00 - 3.00**

❑ Collectables COL-4502, gold vinyl, 1992 ....**2.00 - 4.00**

❑ Sun 217, red vinyl, "DRE1 3054" in trail-off wax, from box "Elvis
   #1 Hit Singles Collection," 2001 ....**2.00 - 4.00**

❑ Sun 217, picture sleeve, "Sun ® Records is a registered
   trademark" on rear along lower left edge, 2001 .....**2.00 - 4.00**

Big Boss Man/Paralyzed

❑ Collectables COL-4521, black vinyl, 1986 .... **1.00 - 3.00**

❑ Collectables COL-4521, gold vinyl, 1992 .... **2.00 - 4.00**

Big Boss Man/You Don't Know Me

❑ RCA Victor 47-9341, black label, dog on left, 1967 .. **5.00 - 10.00**

❑ RCA Victor 47-9341, white label promo, "Not for Sale"
on label, 1967 ....**20.00 - 40.00**

❑ RCA Victor 47-9341, picture sleeve, 1967 .... **12.50 - 25.00**

❑ RCA Victor 447-0662, red label, 1970 .... **5.00 - 10.00**

❑ RCA 447-0662, black label, dog near top, no "Victor"
on label, 1977 ....**2.00 - 4.00**

A Big Hunk o'Love/My Wish Came True

☐ RCA Victor 47-7600, black label, dog on top, 1959 **12.50 - 25.00**

☐ RCA Victor 47-7600, picture sleeve, 1959 ....**35.00 - 70.00**

☐ RCA Victor 447-0626, black label, dog on top, 1962 **7.50 - 15.00**

❑ RCA Victor 447-0626, black label, dog on left,
   1965..**5.00 - 10.00**

❑ RCA Victor 447-0626, orange label, 1969...........**12.50 - 25.00**

❑ RCA Victor 447-0626, red label, 1970..................**4.00 - 8.00**

❑ RCA 447-0626, black label, dog near top,
   no "Victor" on label, 1977 ....**2.00 - 4.00**

❑ Collectables COL-4508, black vinyl, 1986...............**1.00 - 3.00**

❑ Collectables COL-4508, gold vinyl, 1992 ....**2.00 - 4.00**

❑ RCA Victor 47-7600, black label, dog on top,
   red vinyl, "DRC-13043" in trail-off wax,
   from box "Elvis #1 Hit Singles Collection,"
   2001...**2.00 - 4.00**

❑ RCA Victor 47-7600, picture sleeve, "This is a replica
   of the original packaging" on rear at lower left,
   2001...**2.00 - 4.00**

Blue Christmas (same on both sides)

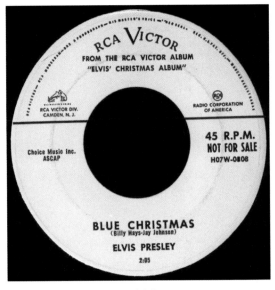

❑ RCA Victor HO7W-0808, white label promo,
   1957... **750.00 – 1,500.**

Blue Christmas/Love Me Tender

❏ RCA 07863-62403-7, silver label, 1992 ....**2.50 - 5.00**

❏ RCA 07863-62403-7, generic white sleeve,
   large hole in middle, with "Elvis --
   The King of Rock 'n' Roll" sticker, 1992 ....**2.50 - 5.00**

Blue Christmas/Santa Claus Is Back in Town

❏ RCA Victor 447-0647, black label,
   dog on left, 1965 ....**6.00 - 12.00**

❏ RCA Victor 447-0647, white label promo,
   "Not for Sale" on label, 1965 ....**20.00 - 40.00**

❏ RCA Victor 447-0647, picture sleeve, has
   "Gold Standard Series" on sleeve, 1965 ....**15.00 - 30.00**

❏ RCA Victor 447-0647, orange label, 1969 ....**12.50 - 25.00**

❏ RCA Victor 447-0647, red label, 1970 ....**4.00 - 8.00**

❏ RCA 447-0647, black label, dog near top,
   no "Victor" on label, 1977 ....**2.00 - 4.00**

❑ RCA 447-0647, picture sleeve, does not mention "Gold Standard
Series" on sleeve, 1977..................................**5.00 - 10.00**

Blue Christmas/Wooden Heart

❑ RCA Victor 447-0720, black label, dog on top,
1964...**7.50 - 15.00**

❑ RCA Victor 447-0720, white label promo, "Not for Sale"
   on label, 1964..**20.00 - 40.00**

❑ RCA Victor 447-0720, picture sleeve, 1964..........**30.00 - 60.00**

❑ RCA Victor 447-0720, black label, dog on top, red vinyl,
   "DRE1 3049" in trail-off wax, from box "Elvis #1 Hit
   Singles Collection," 2001....................................**2.00 - 4.00**

❑ RCA Victor 447-0720, picture sleeve, "This is a replica of the
   original packaging" on rear along left edge, 2001 ..**2.00 - 4.00**

Blue Moon/Just Because

"Picture sleeves" of RCA Victor 47-6640 are bootlegs.

❑ RCA Victor 47-6640, East Coast pressing
   with horizontal line on label, 1956 ....**30.00 - 60.00**

❑ RCA Victor 47-6640, Midwest or West Coast pressing
   with no horizontal line on label, 1956 ....**30.00 - 60.00**

❑ RCA Victor 447-0613, black label, dog on top, 1959 **7.50 - 15.00**

❑ RCA Victor 447-0613, black label, dog on left,
   1965...**5.00 - 10.00**

❑ RCA Victor 447-0613, orange label, 1969 .... **12.50 - 25.00**

❑ RCA Victor 447-0613, red label, 1970 .... **4.00 - 8.00**

❑ RCA 447-0613, black label, dog near top, no "Victor"
   on label, 1977 .... **2.00 - 4.00**

Blue Suede Shoes (same on both sides)

❑ RCA JK-13929, blue vinyl promo, "Not for Sale"
   on label, 1984 .... **12.50 - 25.00**

Blue Suede Shoes/Promised Land

❑ RCA PB-13929, blue vinyl with incorrect label --
   "Blue Suede Shoes" side says "Stereo" and "Promised Land"
   side says "Mono", 1984 .... **7.50 - 15.00**

❑ RCA PB-13929, blue vinyl with correct label --
   "Blue Suede Shoes" side says "Mono" and "Promised Land"
   side says "Stereo", 1984 .... **6.00 - 12.00**

❑ RCA PB-13929, picture sleeve, 1984 .... **5.00 - 10.00**

Blue Suede Shoes/Tutti Frutti

Other than the 2002 sleeve listed, "picture sleeves" of RCA Victor 47-6636 are bootlegs.

❑ RCA Victor 47-6636, East Coast pressing
   with horizontal line on label, 1956 ....**40.00 - 80.00**

❑ RCA Victor 47-6636, Midwest or West Coast pressing
   with no horizontal line on label, 1956 ....**40.00 - 80.00**

❑ RCA Victor 447-0609, black label, dog on top, 1959 **7.50 - 15.00**

❑ RCA Victor 447-0609, black label, dog on left, 1965 **5.00 - 10.00**

❑ RCA Victor 447-0609, orange label, 1969 ....**12.50 - 25.00**

❑ RCA Victor 447-0609, red label, 1970..................**4.00 - 8.00**

❑ RCA 447-0609, black label, dog near top,
   no "Victor" on label, 1977 ....**2.00 - 4.00**

❑ RCA PB-11107, from boxes "15 Golden Records,
   30 Golden Hits" and "20 Golden Hits in
   Full Color Sleeves," 1977 ....**2.00 - 4.00**

❑ RCA PB-11107, picture sleeve, 1977.....................**2.00 - 4.00**

❑ RCA PB-13885, from box "Elvis' Greatest Hits, Golden Singles,
   Volume 1"; gold vinyl, 1984.............................**2.00 - 4.00**

❏ RCA PB-13885, picture sleeve, 1984................**2.00 - 4.00**

❏ RCA Victor 47-6636, black label, dog on top, red vinyl,
   "DRE 13222" in trail-off wax, from box
   "Elvis Hit Singles Collection, Volume 2," 2002.......**2.00 - 4.00**

❏ RCA Victor 47-6636, picture sleeve, "This is a replica
   of the original packaging" on rear along lower
   right edge, though no prior sleeve was legitimately
   made, 2002 ....**2.00 - 4.00**

Bossa Nova Baby/Such a Night

❏ Collectables COL-4513, black vinyl, 1986...............**1.00 - 3.00**

❏ Collectables COL-4513, gold vinyl, 1992 ....**2.00 - 4.00**

Bossa Nova Baby/Witchcraft

❑ RCA Victor 47-8243, black label, dog on top, 1963 .. **6.00 - 12.00**

❑ RCA Victor 47-8243, picture sleeve, "Coming Soon! Special!
   'Fun in Acapulco' LP Album" on sleeve, 1963 ....**15.00 - 30.00**

❑ RCA Victor 47-8243, picture sleeve,

"Ask For 'Fun in Acapulco' LP Album"
on sleeve, 1963...**15.00 - 30.00**

❏ RCA Victor 47-8243, picture sleeve,
   no reference to another album on sleeve,
   1963..**150.00 - 300.00**

❏ RCA Victor 447-0642, black label, dog on top,
   1964...**12.50 - 25.00**

❏ RCA Victor 447-0642, black label, dog on left,
   1965...**5.00 - 10.00**

❏ RCA Victor 447-0642, orange label, 1969...........**12.50 - 25.00**

❏ RCA Victor 447-0642, red label, 1970...................**4.00 - 8.00**

❏ RCA 447-0642, black label, dog near top,
   no "Victor" on label, 1977............................**2.00 - 4.00**

❏ RCA Victor 47-8243, black label, dog on top, red vinyl,
   "DRE 13221" in trail-off wax, from box "Elvis Hit Singles
   Collection, Volume 2," 2002............................**2.00 - 4.00**

❏ RCA Victor 47-8243, picture sleeve, *"Coming Soon! Special! '
   Fun in Acapulco"* LP Album" on sleeve,
   "This is a replica of the original packaging"
   on rear at bottom, 2002...............................**2.00 - 4.00**

Bringing It Back/Pieces of My Life

❏ RCA Victor JA-10401, yellow label promo, both sides
are mono, 1975 ....**12.50 - 25.00**

❏ RCA Victor PB-10401, orange label, 1975 .... **100.00 - 200.00**

❏ RCA Victor PB-10401, tan label, 1975 ....**2.50 - 5.00**

❏ RCA Victor PB-10401, picture sleeve, 1975............ **5.00 - 10.00**

Burning Love/It's a Matter of Time

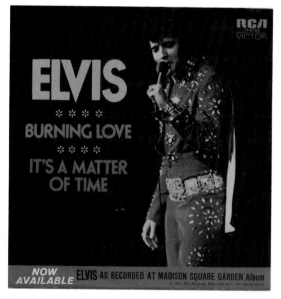

❑ RCA Victor 74-0769, orange label original, 1972......**3.00 - 6.00**

❑ RCA Victor 74-0769, yellow label promo, "Not for Sale"
  on label, 1972...**12.50 - 25.00**

❑ RCA Victor 74-0769, picture sleeve, 1972 .... **7.50 - 15.00**

❑ RCA Victor 74-0769, gray label reissue, 1974...... **75.00 - 150.00**

❑ RCA Victor 74-0769, orange label, red vinyl,
  "DRE 13234" in trail-off wax, from box
  "Elvis Hit Singles Collection, Volume 2," 2002 ...... **2.00 - 4.00**

❑ RCA Victor 74-0769, picture sleeve, "This is a replica
  of the original packaging" on rear along
  lower right edge, 2002 .... **2.00 - 4.00**

Burning Love/Steamroller Blues

❑ RCA Victor GB-10156, Gold Standard Series;
  red label, 1975 .... **4.00 - 8.00**

❑ RCA GB-10156, Gold Standard Series;
  black label, 1977...................................... **2.00 - 4.00**

Can't Help Falling in Love/Rock-a-Hula Baby

❑ RCA Victor 37-7968, "Compact Single 33"
(small hole, plays at LP speed), 1961 ....**1,500 – 2,000**

❑ RCA Victor 37-7968, picture sleeve, must have "Compact
33 Single" and "37-7968" on sleeve, 1961 ....**3,000 – 4,000**

❏ RCA Victor 47-7968, black label, dog on top,
1961 ....**10.00 - 20.00**

❏ RCA Victor 47-7968, picture sleeve, 1961 ....**20.00 - 40.00**

❏ RCA Victor 447-0635, black label, dog on top,
1962 ....**6.00 - 12.00**

❏ RCA Victor 447-0635, black label, dog on left,
1965 ....**5.00 - 10.00**

❏ RCA Victor 447-0635, orange label, 1969 ....**12.50 - 25.00**

❏ RCA Victor 447-0635, red label, 1970 ....**4.00 - 8.00**

❏ RCA 447-0635, black label, dog near top, "Victor"
not on label, 1977 ....**2.00 - 4.00**

❏ RCA PB-11102, from boxes "15 Golden Records, 30 Golden Hits"
and "20 Golden Hits in Full Color Sleeves," 1977 ....**2.00 - 4.00**

❏ RCA PB-11102, picture sleeve, 1977 ....**2.00 - 4.00**

❏ RCA 47-7968, black label, dog near top, no "Victor" on label,
red vinyl, "DRE 13241" in trail-off wax, from box
"Elvis Hit Singles Collection, Volume 2," 2002 ....**2.00 - 4.00**

❏ RCA Victor 47-7968, picture sleeve, "This is a replica
of the original packaging" on back along
lower left edge, 2002 ....**2.00 - 4.00**

Clean Up Your Own Back Yard/The Fair Is Moving On

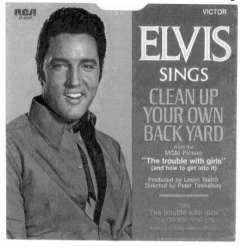

❑ RCA Victor 47-9747, orange label, 1969 .... **4.00 - 8.00**

❑ RCA Victor 47-9747, yellow label promo, "Not for Sale"
on label, 1969 .... **15.00 - 30.00**

❑ RCA Victor 47-9747, picture sleeve, 1969 .... **10.00 - 20.00**

❑ RCA Victor 447-0672, red label, 1970 .... **4.00 - 8.00**

❑ RCA 447-0672, black label, dog near top, no "Victor"
on label, 1977 .... **2.00 - 4.00**

Crying in the Chapel/I Believe in the Man in the Sky

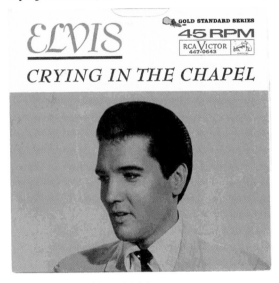

❑ RCA Victor 447-0643, black label,
  dog on left, 1965 .... **5.00 - 10.00**

❑ RCA Victor 447-0643, white label promo, "Not for Sale"
  on label, 1965 .... **15.00 - 30.00**

- ❏ RCA Victor 447-0643, picture sleeve, 1965 ....**15.00 - 30.00**

- ❏ RCA Victor 447-0643, red label, 1970 ....**4.00 - 8.00**

- ❏ RCA 447-0643, black label, dog near top,
  no "Victor" on label, 1977 ....**2.00 - 4.00**

- ❏ RCA PB-11113, from box "15 Golden Records,
  30 Golden Hits," 1977 ....**2.00 - 4.00**

- ❏ RCA PB-11113, picture sleeve, 1977 ....**2.00 - 4.00**

- ❏ Collectables 80003, gray marbled vinyl, 1997 ....**2.00 - 4.00**

Do the Clam/You'll Be Gone

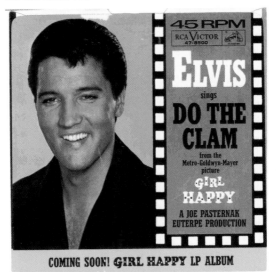

❑ RCA Victor 47-8500, black label, dog on top, 1965 .. **5.00 - 10.00**

❑ RCA Victor 47-8500, white label promo,
  "Not for Sale" on label, 1965 ....**25.00 - 50.00**

❑ RCA Victor 47-8500, picture sleeve, 1965 ....**12.50 - 25.00**

❑ RCA Victor 447-0648, black label,
 dog on left, 1965...**5.00 - 10.00**

❑ RCA Victor 447-0648, red label, 1970.................**5.00 - 10.00**

❑ RCA 447-0648, black label, dog near top,
 no "Victor" on label, 1977...............................**2.00 - 4.00**

Don't Be Cruel/Ain't That Lovin' You Baby (Fast Version)

❑ RCA 02783-62402-7, silver label, 1992.................**2.50 - 5.00**

❑ RCA 07863-62402-7, generic white sleeve,
 large hole in middle, with "Elvis --
 The King of Rock 'n' Roll" sticker, 1992...............**2.50 - 5.00**

Don't Be Cruel/Hound Dog

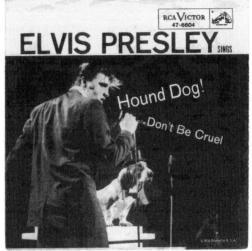

❏ RCA Victor 47-6604, East Coast pressing with horizontal
line on label, 1956....................................**15.00 - 30.00**

❏ RCA Victor 47-6604, Midwest or West Coast pressing
without horizontal line on label, 1956 ....**15.00 - 30.00**

❏ RCA Victor 47-6604, picture sleeve, "Hound Dog!" listed above
"Don't Be Cruel," 1956 ....**60.00 - 120.00**

❑ RCA Victor 47-6604, picture sleeve, "Don't Be Cruel"
listed above "Hound Dog!", 1956 .... **100.00 - 200.00**

❑ RCA Victor 447-0608, black label, dog on top, 1959 **7.50 - 15.00**

❑ RCA Victor 447-0608, white label promo, "Not for Sale"
on label, 1964 .... **50.00 - 100.00**

❑ RCA Victor 447-0608, picture sleeve, usually found
with promo copies, 1964 .... **100.00 - 200.00**

❏ RCA Victor 447-0608, black label, dog on left, 1965 **5.00 - 10.00**

❏ RCA Victor 447-0608, orange label, 1969 ....**12.50 - 25.00**

❏ RCA Victor 447-0608, red label, 1970 ....**4.00 - 8.00**

❏ RCA 447-0608, black label, dog near top, no "Victor"
on label,1977 ....**2.00 - 4.00**

Don't Cry Daddy/Rubberneckin'

❏ RCA Victor 47-9768, orange label, 1969 ....**4.00 - 8.00**

❏ RCA Victor 47-9768, yellow label promo, "Not for Sale"
on label, 1969 ....**15.00 - 30.00**

❏ RCA Victor 47-9768, picture sleeve, 1969 .... **7.50 - 15.00**

❏ RCA Victor 447-0674, red label, 1970 ....**4.00 - 8.00**

❏ RCA 447-0674, black label, dog near top, no "Victor"
on label, 1977 ....**2.00 - 4.00**

❏ Collectables 80005, gray marbled vinyl, 1997 ....**2.00 - 4.00**

❏ RCA Victor 47-9768, orange label, red vinyl, "DRE 13224"
in trail-off wax, from box "Elvis Hit Singles Collection,
Volume 2," 2002 ....**2.00 - 4.00**

❏ RCA Victor 47-9768, picture sleeve, "This is a replica
of the original packaging" on rear at
lower right edge, 2002 ....**2.00 - 4.00**

Don't/I Beg of You

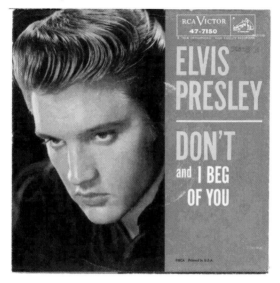

❑ RCA Victor 47-7150, black label, dog on top, 1958.. **7.50 - 15.00**

❑ RCA Victor 47-7150, picture sleeve, 1958 ....**45.00 - 90.00**

❑ RCA Victor 447-0621, black label, dog on top,
     1961.. **6.00 - 12.00**

❑ RCA Victor 447-0621, black label, dog on left, 1965 **5.00 - 10.00**

❑ RCA Victor 447-0621, orange label, 1969 ....**12.50 - 25.00**

❑ RCA Victor 447-0621, red label, 1970 ....**4.00 - 8.00**

❑ RCA 447-0621, black label, dog near top, no "Victor"
on label, 1977 ....**2.00 - 4.00**

❑ Collectables 80004, gray marbled vinyl, 1997 ....**2.00 - 4.00**

❑ RCA Victor 47-7150, black label, dog on top, red vinyl,
"DRC-13041" in trail-off wax, from box "Elvis #1 Hit
Singles Collection," 2001 ....**2.00 - 4.00**

❑ RCA Victor 47-7150, picture sleeve, "This is a replica of the
original packaging" on rear at lower right, 2001....**2.00 - 4.00**

Don't/Wear My Ring Around Your Neck

❑ RCA Victor SP-45-76, promo only; black label, dog on top,
"Not for Sale" on label, 1960 ....**400.00 - 800.00**

❑ RCA Victor SP-45-76, picture sleeve, 1960 ....**1,500 – 2,000**

Easy Question/It Feels So Right
See (Such An) Easy Question/It Feels So Right.

Elvis #1 Hit Singles Collection

❏ Collectables COL-0103, contains reproductions,
on red vinyl, of 18 RCA singles and all five Sun singles,
using facsimiles of original labels and reproductions
of original picture sleeves, and all-new sleeves
for those songs not issued originally with picture sleeves;
with poster and all in wooden box, 2001.........**50.00 - 100.00**

Elvis Hit Singles Collection Volume 2

❏ Collectables COL-0134, contains reproductions,
on red vinyl, of 23 RCA singles not in the first box,
using facsimiles of original labels and reproductions
of original picture sleeves, and all-new sleeves
for those songs not issued originally with picture sleeves;
with poster and all in wooden box, 2002.........**50.00 - 100.00**

The Elvis Medley (Long Version)/(Short Version)

❏ RCA JB-13351, promo only on gold vinyl,
1982...**150.00 - 300.00**

❏ RCA JB-13351, promo only on black vinyl,
1982...**7.50 - 15.00**

The Elvis Medley/Always on My Mind

❑ RCA PB-13351, black label, dog near top, 1982........**2.50 - 5.00**

❑ RCA PB-13351, picture sleeve, 1982....................**5.00 - 10.00**

❑ Collectables COL-4564, black vinyl, 1986.............**1.00 - 3.00**

❑ Collectables COL-4564, gold vinyl, 1992 ....**2.00 - 4.00**

Elvis' Greatest Hits, Golden Singles, Volume 1

❏ RCA PB-13897, box set of six 45s with sleeves (13885-13890); with box, 1984 .... **7.50 - 15.00**

Elvis' Greatest Hits, Golden Singles, Volume 2

❏ RCA PB-13898, box set of six 45s with sleeves (13891-13896); with box, 1984 .... **7.50 - 15.00**

15 Golden Records, 30 Golden Hits

❏ RCA PP-11301, includes 15 records with sleeves (11099-11113) and outer box, 1977 .... **30.00 - 60.00**

Follow That Dream/
When My Blue Moon Turns to Gold Again

❏ Collectables COL-4515, black vinyl, 1986 .... **1.00 - 3.00**

❏ Collectables COL-4515, gold vinyl, 1992 .... **2.00 - 4.00**

A Fool Such As I/I Need Your Love Tonight

See (NOW AND THEN THERE'S) A FOOL SUCH AS I/I NEED YOUR LOVE TONIGHT.

Fools Fall in Love/Blue Suede Shoes

❏ Collectables COL-4522, black vinyl, 1986 .... **1.00 - 3.00**

❏ Collectables COL-4522, gold vinyl, 1992 .... **2.00 - 4.00**

Frankie and Johnny/Love Letters

❏ Collectables COL-4516, black vinyl, 1986 .... **1.00 - 3.00**

❏ Collectables COL-4516, gold vinyl, 1992 .... **2.00 - 4.00**

Frankie and Johnny/Please Don't Stop Loving Me

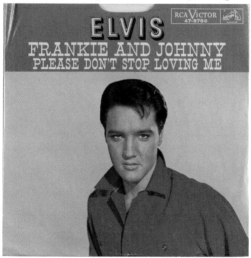

❑ RCA Victor 47-8780, black label, dog on left,
   1966...**5.00 - 10.00**

❑ RCA Victor 47-8780, white label promo,
   "Not for Sale" on label, 1966........................**25.00 - 50.00**

❑ RCA Victor 47-8780, picture sleeve, 1966 ....**12.50 - 25.00**

❑ RCA Victor 447-0656, black label, dog on left, 1968 **5.00 - 10.00**

❑ RCA Victor 447-0656, orange label, 1969...........**12.50 - 25.00**

❑ RCA Victor 447-0656, red label, 1970....................**4.00 - 8.00**

❑ RCA 447-0656, black label, dog near top,
   no "Victor" on label, 1977 ....**2.00 - 4.00**

Girls! Girls! Girls!/Ain't That Loving You Baby

❑ Collectables COL-4743, 1997 ....**1.00 - 3.00**

Good Luck Charm/Anything That's Part of You

❏ RCA Victor 37-7992, "Compact Single 33"
(small hole, plays at LP speed), 1962..............**1,750 – 2,500**

❏ RCA Victor 37-7992, picture sleeve, must have "Compact
33 Single" and "37-7992" on sleeve, 1962........**3,500 – 5,000**

❏ RCA Victor 47-7992, black label, dog on top, 1962. **10.00 - 20.00**

❏ RCA Victor 47-7992, picture sleeve, titles in blue and
   pink letters, 1962 ....**20.00 - 40.00**

❏ RCA Victor 47-7992, picture sleeve, titles in rust and
   lavender letters, 1962 ....**20.00 - 40.00**

❏ RCA Victor 447-0636, black label, dog on top,
   1962...**6.00 - 12.00**

❏ RCA Victor 447-0636, black label, dog on left, 1965 **5.00 - 10.00**

❏ RCA Victor 447-0636, orange label, 1969 ....**12.50 - 25.00**

❏ RCA Victor 447-0636, red label, 1970....................**4.00 - 8.00**

❏ RCA 447-0636, black label, dog near top, no "Victor"
   on label, 1977 ....**2.00 - 4.00**

❏ Collectables 80006, gray marbled vinyl, 1997.........**2.00 - 4.00**

❏ RCA Victor 47-7992, black label, dog on top, red vinyl,
   "DRE1 3045" in trail-off wax, from box "Elvis #1 Hit
   Singles Collection," 2001.....................................**2.00 - 4.00**

❏ RCA Victor 47-7992, picture sleeve, titles in rust and
   lavender letters, "This is a replica of the original
   packaging" on rear at lower left edge, 2001 ....**2.00 - 4.00**

Good Rockin' Tonight/
I Don't Care If the Sun Don't Shine

Other than the 2001 sleeve listed, "picture sleeves" of Sun 210 and RCA Victor 47-6381 are bootlegs.

- ❏ Sun 210, 1954 (beware of counterfeits)............**2,000. – 3,500**

- ❏ RCA Victor 47-6381, East Coast pressing with horizontal line on label, 1955...................................**30.00 - 60.00**

❏ RCA Victor 47-6381, Midwest or West Coast pressing without
   horizontal line on label, 1955......................**30.00 - 60.00**

❏ RCA Victor 447-0602, black label, dog on top, 1959 **7.50 - 15.00**

❏ RCA Victor 447-0602, one-of-a-kind after-hours red
   vinyl pressing, 1959...................................**4,000 – 6,000**

❏ RCA Victor 447-0602, white label promo, "Not for Sale" on label,
   1964..**50.00 - 100.00**

❏ RCA Victor 447-0602, picture sleeve, usually found
   with promo copies, 1964 ....**100.00 - 200.00**

❏ RCA Victor 447-0602, black label, dog on left, 1965 **5.00 - 10.00**

❏ RCA Victor 447-0602, red label, 1970...................**4.00 - 8.00**

❏ RCA 447-0602, black label, dog near top, no "Victor"
   on label, 1977...**2.00 - 4.00**

❏ Collectables COL-4500, black vinyl, 1986...............**1.00 - 3.00**

❏ Collectables COL-4500, gold vinyl, 1992 ....**2.00 - 4.00**

❏ Sun 210, red vinyl, "DRE1 3052" in trail-off wax,
   from box "Elvis #1 Hit Singles Collection," 2001 ....**2.00 - 4.00**

❏ Sun 210, picture sleeve, "Sun ® Records is a registered
   trademark" on rear along lower left edge, 2001 .....**2.00 - 4.00**

Guitar Man (mono/stereo)

❑ RCA JH-12158, promo only on black vinyl, 1981 .... **7.50 - 15.00**

❑ RCA JH-12158, promo only on red vinyl, 1981 .. **150.00 - 300.00**

Guitar Man/Faded Love

❑ RCA PB-12158, 1981...**2.50 - 5.00**

❑ RCA PB-12158, picture sleeve, 1981...................**5.00 - 10.00**

Guitar Man/High Heel Sneakers

❑ RCA Victor 47-9425, black label, dog on top, 1968 .. **5.00 - 10.00**

❑ RCA Victor 47-9425, yellow label promo, "Not for Sale"
on label, 1968...**15.00 - 30.00**

❑ RCA Victor 47-9425, picture sleeve, *"Coming Soon Elvis' Gold
Records Volume 4"* on sleeve, 1968...................**12.50 - 25.00**

❑ RCA Victor 47-9425, picture sleeve, *"Ask For Elvis' Gold Records
Volume 4"* on sleeve, 1968..............................**12.50 - 25.00**

❑ RCA Victor 447-0663, red label, 1970...................**4.00 - 8.00**

❑ RCA 447-0663, black label, dog near top,
no "Victor" on label, 1977 ....**2.00 - 4.00**

❑ Collectables 80007, gray marbled vinyl, 1997..........**2.00 - 4.00**

Hard Headed Woman/Don't Ask Me Why

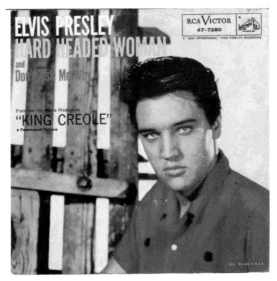

❏ RCA Victor 47-7280, black label, dog on top,
1958...**12.50 - 25.00**

❏ RCA Victor 47-7280, picture sleeve, 1958 ....**35.00 - 70.00**

❑ RCA Victor 447-0623, black label, dog on top,
   1961..**7.50 - 15.00**

❑ RCA Victor 447-0623, black label, dog on left,
   1965..**5.00 - 10.00**

❑ RCA Victor 447-0623, orange label, 1969...........**12.50 - 25.00**

❑ RCA Victor 447-0623, red label, 1970...................**4.00 - 8.00**

❑ RCA 447-0623, black label, dog near top, no "Victor"
   on label, 1977..**2.00 - 4.00**

❑ Collectables 80008, gray marbled vinyl, 1997..........**2.00 - 4.00**

❑ RCA Victor 47-7280, black label, dog on top, red vinyl,
   "DRE-13042" in trail-off wax, from box "Elvis #1 Hit
   Singles Collection," 2001.................................**2.00 - 4.00**

❑ RCA Victor 47-7280, picture sleeve, "This is a replica
   of the original packaging" on rear along right edge,
   2001..**2.00 - 4.00**

He Touched Me/The Bosom of Abraham

❏ RCA Victor 74-0651, orange label, with mispressed version
of "He Touched Me" that, at 45 rpm, sounds fast;
to match the correct version, the record should
be played at around 35 rpm; A-side has "AWKS-1277"
stamped in trail-off wax., 1972...................**75.00 - 150.00**

❑ RCA Victor 74-0651, orange label, with correct
   pressing of "He Touched Me"; A-side has
   "APKS-1277" stamped in trail-off wax., 1972.........**4.00 - 8.00**

❑ RCA Victor 74-0651, yellow label promo, with
   "Not for Sale" on label, A-side has
   "AWKS-1277" stamped in trail-off wax., 1972 ...**60.00 - 120.00**

❑ RCA Victor 74-0651, picture sleeve, 1972 ....**60.00 - 120.00**

Heartbreak Hotel/Heartbreak Hotel

❏ RCA 8760-7-R, red label, B-side by "David Keith & Charlie
Schlatter with Zulu Time," 1988........................**2.50 - 5.00**

❏ RCA 8760-7-R, picture sleeve, stock version with pink Cadillac
pictured, 1988...**3.00 - 6.00**

❑ RCA 8760-7-RA1, white label promo, "Not for Sale" on label, B-side by "David Keith & Charlie Schlatter with Zulu Time," 1988..**12.50 - 25.00**

❑ RCA 8760-7-RA1, picture sleeve, promo version with "The Infamous Butch Waugh as Elvis Presley," 1988...**40.00 - 80.00**

Heartbreak Hotel/Hound Dog

❏ RCA 07863-62449-7, silver label, 1992 .... **2.50 - 5.00**

❏ RCA 07863-62449-7, generic white sleeve,
   large hole in middle, with "Elvis --
   The King of Rock 'n' Roll" sticker, 1992 .... **2.50 - 5.00**

Heartbreak Hotel/I Was the One

Other than the 2001 sleeve listed, "picture sleeves"
of RCA Victor 47-6420 are bootlegs.

❏ RCA Victor 47-6420, East Coast pressing with horizontal
   line on label, 1956 .... **20.00 - 40.00**

❏ RCA Victor 47-6420, Midwest or West Coast pressing
   without horizontal line on label, 1956 .... **20.00 - 40.00**

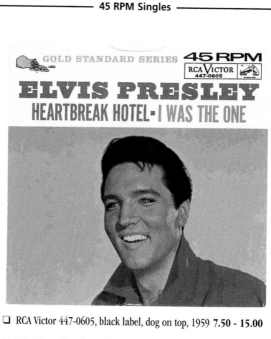

- RCA Victor 447-0605, black label, dog on top, 1959 **7.50 - 15.00**

- RCA Victor 447-0605, white label promo, "Not for Sale" on label, 1964.......................................**50.00 - 100.00**

- RCA Victor 447-0605, picture sleeve, usually found with promo copies, 1964 ....**100.00 - 200.00**

❏ RCA Victor 447-0605, black label, dog on left, 1965 **5.00 - 10.00**

❏ RCA Victor 447-0605, orange label, 1969 ....**12.50 - 25.00**

❏ RCA Victor 447-0605, red label, 1970 ....**4.00 - 8.00**

❏ RCA 447-0605, black label, dog near top, no "Victor" on label, 1977 ....**2.00 - 4.00**

❏ RCA PB-11105, from boxes "15 Golden Records, 30 Golden Hits" and "20 Golden Hits in Full Color Sleeves," 1977 ....**2.00 - 4.00**

❏ RCA PB-11105, picture sleeve, 1977......................**2.00 - 4.00**

❏ Collectables 80009, gray marbled vinyl, 1997..........**2.00 - 4.00**

❏ RCA Victor 47-6420, black label, dog on top, red vinyl, "DRE1 3034" in trail-off wax, from box "Elvis #1 Hit Singles Collection," 2001 ....**2.00 - 4.00**

❏ RCA Victor 47-6420, picture sleeve, "The RCA logo is TMK(s) ® Registered Marca(s) Registrada(s) RCA Corporation" on rear at lower left, 2001 ....**2.00 - 4.00**

Heartbreak Hotel/Jailhouse Rock

❏ RCA PB-13892, from box "Elvis' Greatest Hits, Golden Singles, Volume 2"; gold vinyl, 1984 ....**2.00 - 4.00**

❏ RCA PB-13892, picture sleeve, 1984......................**2.00 - 4.00**

His Latest Flame/Little Sister

See (MARIE'S THE NAME) HIS LATEST FLAME/LITTLE SISTER.

Hound Dog/Don't Be Cruel

See DON'T BE CRUEL/HOUND DOG.

How Great Thou Art/His Hand in Mine

❑ RCA Victor 74-0130, orange label, 1969............**12.50 - 25.00**

❑ RCA Victor 74-0130, yellow label promo, "Not for Sale"
    on label, 1969...**60.00 - 120.00**

❑ RCA Victor 74-0130, picture sleeve, 1969..........**75.00 - 150.00**

❑ RCA Victor 447-0670, red label, 1970..................**5.00 - 10.00**

❑ RCA 447-0670, black label, dog near top, no "Victor"
    on label, 1977...**2.00 - 4.00**

❑ Collectables COL-4520, black vinyl, 1986.............**1.00 - 3.00**

❑ Collectables COL-4520, gold vinyl, 1992.............**2.00 - 4.00**

How Great Thou Art/So High

❑ RCA Victor SP-45-162, white label promo, "Not for Sale"
    on label, 1967..**75.00 - 150.00**

❑ RCA Victor SP-45-162, picture sleeve; counterfeits exist
    but are blurry, 1967................................**100.00 - 200.00**

Hurt/For the Heart

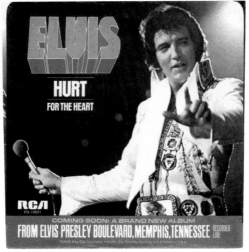

❑ RCA Victor JB-10601, yellow label promo,
"Not for Sale" on label, 1976.......................**12.50 - 25.00**

❑ RCA Victor PB-10601, tan label, 1976.................**2.50 - 5.00**

❑ RCA Victor PB-10601, picture sleeve, 1976...........**5.00 - 10.00**

❑ RCA PB-10601, black label, dog near top, no "Victor"
on label, 1976.......................................**50.00 - 100.00**

I Feel So Bad/Wild in the Country

❑ RCA Victor 37-7880, "Compact Single 33"
    (small hole, plays at LP speed), 1961.......... **500.00 – 1,000.**

❑ RCA Victor 37-7880, picture sleeve, must have "Compact 33
    Single" and "37-7880" on sleeve, 1961........ **600.00 – 1,200.**

❑ RCA Victor 47-7880, black label, dog on top, 1961.**10.00 - 20.00**

❑ RCA Victor 47-7880, picture sleeve, 1961 ....**25.00 - 50.00**

❑ RCA Victor 447-0631, black label, dog on top, 1962 **6.00 - 12.00**

❑ RCA Victor 447-0631, black label, dog on left, 1965 **5.00 - 10.00**

❑ RCA Victor 447-0631, red label, 1970....................**4.00 - 8.00**

❑ RCA 447-0631, black label, dog near top, no "Victor"
    on label, 1977...**2.00 - 4.00**

❑ Collectables COL-4510, black vinyl, 1986...............**1.00 - 3.00**

❑ Collectables COL-4510, gold vinyl, 1992 ....**2.00 - 4.00**

❑ RCA Victor 47-7880, black label, dog on top, red vinyl,
    "DRE 13225" in trail-off wax, from box "Elvis Hit
    Singles Collection, Volume 2," 2002....................**2.00 - 4.00**

❑ RCA Victor 47-7880, picture sleeve, "This is a replica
    of the original packaging" on rear along
    lower right edge, 2002...................................**2.00 - 4.00**

I Forgot to Remember to Forget/Mystery Train

Most sources list "Mystery Train" as the A-side, and perhaps it was, but "I Forgot to Remember to Forget" was the bigger hit when it was first issued, as it got to #1 on the country charts. Other than the 2001 sleeve listed, "picture sleeves" of Sun 223 and RCA Victor 47-6357 are bootlegs.

❑ Sun 223, 1955 (beware of counterfeits)............**1,250 – 2,500**

❑ RCA Victor 47-6357, East Coast pressing with horizontal line
on label, 1955 ....**30.00 - 60.00**

❑ RCA Victor 47-6357, Midwest or West Coast pressing
without horizontal line on label, 1955 ....**30.00 - 60.00**

❑ RCA Victor 47-6357, white label promo, "Record Prevue" on label, 1955 .... **200.00 - 400.00**

❑ RCA Victor 447-0600, black label, dog on top, 1959 **7.50 - 15.00**

❑ RCA Victor 447-0600, black label, dog on left, 1965 **5.00 - 10.00**

❑ RCA Victor 447-0600, orange label, 1969 ....**12.50 - 25.00**

❑ RCA Victor 447-0600, red label, 1970...............**4.00 - 8.00**

❑ RCA 447-0600, black label, dog near top, "Victor" not
on label, 1977...............**2.00 - 4.00**

❑ Collectables 80010, gray marbled vinyl, 1997..........**2.00 - 4.00**

❑ Sun 223, red vinyl, "DRE-1-3055" in trail-off wax, from box
"Elvis #1 Hit Singles Collection," 2001...............**2.00 - 4.00**

❑ Sun 223, picture sleeve, "Sun ® Records is a registered
trademark" on rear along bottom, 2001..............**2.00 - 4.00**

I Got a Woman/I'm Counting On You

"Picture sleeves" of RCA Victor 47-6637 are bootlegs.

❑ RCA Victor 47-6637, East Coast pressing with
horizontal line on label, 1956.......................**40.00 - 80.00**

❑ RCA Victor 47-6637, Midwest or West Coast pressing
without horizontal line on label, 1956.............**40.00 - 80.00**

❑ RCA Victor 447-0610, black label, dog on top, 1959 **7.50 - 15.00**

❑ Collectables COL-4503, black vinyl, 1986...............**1.00 - 3.00**

❑ Collectables COL-4503, gold vinyl, 1992...............**2.00 - 4.00**

I Really Don't Want to Know/ There Goes My Everything

❑ RCA Victor 47-9960, orange label, 1971 .... **3.00 - 6.00**

❑ RCA Victor 47-9960, picture sleeve, with "Coming Soon – New Album" on sleeve, 1971 .... **7.50 - 15.00**

❑ RCA Victor 47-9960, picture sleeve, with "Now Available – New Album" on sleeve, 1971 .... **7.50 - 15.00**

❑ RCA Victor 447-0679, red label, 1972 .... **4.00 - 8.00**

❑ RCA 447-0679, black label, dog near top, no "Victor" on label, 1977 .... **2.00 - 4.00**

❑ Collectables 80012, gray marbled vinyl, 1997 .... **2.00 - 4.00**

I Want You, I Need You, I Love You/Love Me

❑ RCA PB-13887, from box "Elvis' Greatest Hits, Golden Singles, Volume 1"; gold vinyl, 1984 .... **2.00 - 4.00**

❑ RCA PB-13887, picture sleeve, 1984 .... **2.00 - 4.00**

I Want You, I Need You, I Love You/My Baby Left Me

Other than the 2001 sleeve listed, "picture sleeves" of RCA Victor 47-6540 are bootlegs.

❑ RCA Victor 47-6540, East Coast pressing
  with horizontal line on label, 1956 ....**20.00 - 40.00**

❑ RCA Victor 47-6540, Midwest or West Coast pressing
  without horizontal line on label, 1956 ....**20.00 - 40.00**

❑ RCA Victor 447-0607, black label, dog on top, 1959 **7.50 - 15.00**

❑ RCA Victor 447-0607, black label, dog on left, 1965 **5.00 - 10.00**

❑ RCA Victor 447-0607, orange label, 1969 ....**12.50 - 25.00**

❑ RCA Victor 447-0607, red label, 1970 ....**4.00 - 8.00**

❑ RCA 447-0607, black label, dog near top, no "Victor"
  on label, 1977 ....**2.00 - 4.00**

❑ Collectables 80013, gray marbled vinyl, 1997 ....**2.00 - 4.00**

❑ RCA Victor 47-6540, black label, dog on top, red vinyl,
  "DRE-13056" in trail-off wax, from box "Elvis #1 Hit Singles
  Collection," 2001 ....**2.00 - 4.00**

❑ RCA Victor 47-6540, picture sleeve, "The RCA logo is TMK(s) ®
  Registered Marca(s) Registrada(s) RCA Corporation" on rear at
  lower left, 2001 ....**2.00 - 4.00**

I Was the One/Wear My Ring Around Your Neck

❑ RCA JB-13500, promo only on gold vinyl, 1983. **150.00 - 300.00**

❑ RCA JB-13500, promo, black vinyl, 1983............... **7.50 - 15.00**

❑ RCA PB-13500, black label, dog near top, 1983........ **2.50 - 5.00**

❑ RCA PB-13500, picture sleeve, 1983.................... **5.00 - 10.00**

I'll Be Back (b-side blank)

❏ RCA Victor 4-834-115, one-sided promo with designation "For Special Academy Consideration Only", 1966......**6,000 – 8,000**

I'll Never Let You Go (Little Darlin')/I'm Gonna Sit Right Down and Cry (Over You)

"Picture sleeves" of RCA Victor 47-6638 are bootlegs.

❏ RCA Victor 47-6638, East Coast pressing with horizontal line on label, 1956...**35.00 - 70.00**

❏ RCA Victor 47-6638, Midwest or West Coast pressing without horizontal line on label, 1956.......................**35.00 - 70.00**

❏ RCA Victor 447-0611, black label, dog on top, 1959 **7.50 - 15.00**

❏ Collectables COL-4504, black vinyl, 1986..............**1.00 - 3.00**

❏ Collectables COL-4504, gold vinyl, 1992 ....**2.00 - 4.00**

I'm Leavin'/Heart of Rome

❑ RCA Victor 47-9998, orange label, 1971.................**3.00 - 6.00**

❑ RCA Victor 47-9998, yellow label promo, "Not for Sale" on label, 1971...**12.50 - 25.00**

❑ RCA Victor 47-9998, picture sleeve, 1971 ....**10.00 - 20.00**

❏ RCA Victor 447-0683, red label, 1972.................**4.00 - 8.00**

❏ RCA 447-0683, black label, dog near top, no "Victor"
  on label, 1977...**2.00 - 4.00**

I'm Yours/(It's a) Long, Lonely Highway

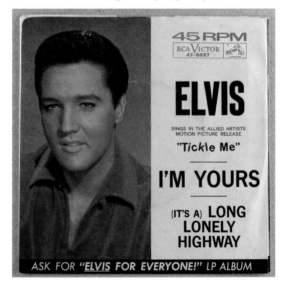

❏ RCA Victor 47-8657, black label, dog on left, 1965.. **5.00 - 10.00**

❏ RCA Victor 47-8657, white label promo, "Not for Sale"
on label, 1965 ....**20.00 - 40.00**

❏ RCA Victor 47-8657, picture sleeve, 1965 ....**12.50 - 25.00**

❏ RCA Victor 447-0654, black label, dog on left, 1966 **5.00 - 10.00**

❏ RCA Victor 447-0654, red label, 1970...................**4.00 - 8.00**

❏ RCA 447-0654, black label, dog near top, no "Victor"
on label, 1977 ....**2.00 - 4.00**

❏ RCA Victor 47-8657, black label, dog on left, red vinyl,
"DRE 13233" in trail-off wax, from box "Elvis Hit Singles
Collection, Volume 2," 2002 ....**2.00 - 4.00**

❏ RCA Victor 47-8657, picture sleeve, "This is a replica of the
original packaging" on rear at bottom, 2002 ....**2.00 - 4.00**

I've Lost You/The Next Step Is Love

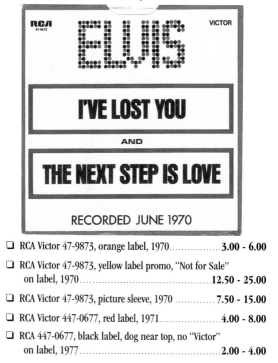

- ❑ RCA Victor 47-9873, orange label, 1970.................**3.00 - 6.00**
- ❑ RCA Victor 47-9873, yellow label promo, "Not for Sale" on label, 1970...**12.50 - 25.00**
- ❑ RCA Victor 47-9873, picture sleeve, 1970 ....**7.50 - 15.00**
- ❑ RCA Victor 447-0677, red label, 1971..................**4.00 - 8.00**
- ❑ RCA 447-0677, black label, dog near top, no "Victor" on label, 1977..**2.00 - 4.00**

If Every Day Was Like Christmas/
How Would You Like to Be

- ❏ RCA Victor 47-8950, black label, dog on left, 1966 **10.00 - 20.00**
- ❏ RCA Victor 47-8950, white label promo, "Not for Sale" on label, 1966 ....**25.00 - 50.00**
- ❏ RCA Victor 47-8950, picture sleeve, 1966 ....**20.00 - 40.00**
- ❏ RCA Victor 447-0681, red label, 1972 ....**4.00 - 8.00**
- ❏ RCA 447-0681, black label, dog near top, no "Victor" on label, 1977 ....**2.00 - 4.00**

If I Can Dream/Edge of Reality

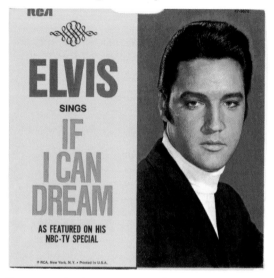

❏ RCA Victor 47-9670, orange label, 1968 .... **4.00 - 8.00**

❏ RCA Victor 47-9670, yellow label promo, "Not for Sale"
on label, 1968 .... **15.00 - 30.00**

❑ RCA Victor 47-9670, picture sleeve,
   "As Featured on His NBC-TV Special"
   on sleeve, 1968 ....**10.00 - 20.00**

❑ RCA Victor 47-9670, picture sleeve,
   with no memtion of his NBC-TV special on sleeve,
   1969..**10.00 - 20.00**

❑ RCA Victor 447-0668, red label, 1970...................**4.00 - 8.00**

❑ RCA 447-0668, black label, dog near top,
   no "Victor" on label, 1977 ....**2.00 - 4.00**

❑ Collectables 80014, gray marbled vinyl, 1997.........**2.00 - 4.00**

❑ RCA Victor 47-9670, orange label, red vinyl,
   "DRE 13229" in trail-off wax, from box
   "Elvis Hit Singles Collection,
   Volume 2," 2002 ....**2.00 - 4.00**

❑ RCA Victor 47-9670, picture sleeve,
   with no memtion of his NBC-TV special on sleeve,
   "This is a replica of the original packaging"
   on rear at lower left, 2002 ....**2.00 - 4.00**

If You Talk in Your Sleep/Help Me

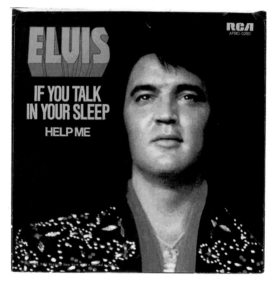

❑ RCA Victor APBO-0280, orange label, with
   "If You Talk" on one line and "In Your Sleep"
   on a second line on label, 1974..........................**3.00 - 6.00**

❏ RCA Victor APBO-0280, orange label, with
"If You Talk in Your Sleep" all on one line
on label, 1974 .... **6.00 - 12.00**

❏ RCA Victor APBO-0280, picture sleeve, 1974 .... **7.50 - 15.00**

❏ RCA Victor DJAO-0280, light yellow label promo,
"Not for Sale" on label, both sides mono, 1974 ... **12.50 - 25.00**

The Impossible Dream (The Quest)/
An American Trilogy

❏ RCA JH-13302, gold label, "Not for Sale" and
"In Commemoration, Tupelo, Mississippi,
August 16, 1982" on label, 1982 .... **50.00 - 100.00**

❏ RCA JH-13302, picture sleeve; the record and sleeve
were distributed to visitors to Elvis' birthplace in Tupelo,
Mississippi, 1982 .... **50.00 - 100.00**

In the Ghetto/Any Day Now

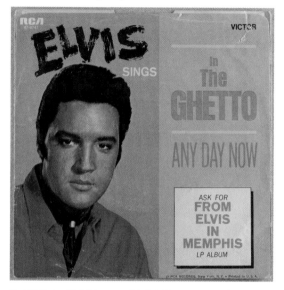

❑ RCA Victor 47-9741, orange label, 1969..............**4.00 - 8.00**

❑ RCA Victor 47-9741, yellow label promo, "Not for Sale"
on label, 1969...**15.00 - 30.00**

❑ RCA Victor 47-9741, picture sleeve, *"Coming Soon From Elvis in Memphis LP Album"* on sleeve, 1969............**10.00 - 20.00**

❑ RCA Victor 47-9741, picture sleeve, *"Ask For From Elvis in Memphis LP Album"* on sleeve, 1969............**10.00 - 20.00**

❑ RCA Victor 447-0671, red label, 1970............**4.00 - 8.00**

❑ RCA 447-0671, black label, dog near top, no "Victor" on label, 1977............**2.00 - 4.00**

❑ RCA PB-11100, from boxes "15 Golden Records, 30 Golden Hits" and "20 Golden Hits in Full Color Sleeves," 1977....**2.00 - 4.00**

❑ RCA PB-11100, picture sleeve, 1977............**2.00 - 4.00**

❑ RCA Victor 47-9741, orange label, red vinyl, "DRE 13239" in trail-off wax, from box "Elvis Hit Singles Collection, Volume 2," 2002............**2.00 - 4.00**

❑ RCA Victor 47-9741, picture sleeve, *"Ask For From Elvis in Memphis LP Album"* on sleeve, "This is a replica of the original packaging" on rear at lower right. 2002 ...**2.00 - 4.00**

In the Ghetto/If I Can Dream

❑ RCA PB-13890, from box "Elvis' Greatest Hits, Golden Singles, Volume 1"; gold vinyl, 1984............**2.00 - 4.00**

❑ RCA PB-13890, picture sleeve, 1984............**2.00 - 4.00**

Indescribably Blue/Fools Fall in Love

❑ RCA Victor 47-9056, black label, dog on left, 1966.. **5.00 - 10.00**

❑ RCA Victor 47-9056, white label promo, "Not for Sale"
on label, 1966..**20.00 - 40.00**

❑ RCA Victor 47-9056, picture sleeve, 1966 ....**12.50 - 25.00**

❑ RCA Victor 447-0659, orange label, 1969 ....**12.50 - 25.00**

❑ RCA Victor 447-0659, red label, 1970...................**4.00 - 8.00**

❑ RCA 447-0659, black label, dog near top, no "Victor"
on label, 1977..**2.00 - 4.00**

It's Now or Never/A Mess of Blues

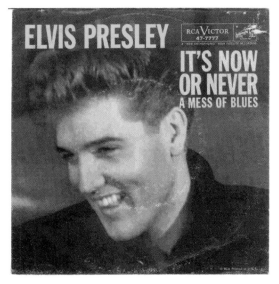

❏ RCA Victor 47-7777, black label, dog on top, with alternate
mix of "It's Now of Never" that is missing the piano overdub;
known copies have "L2WW-0100-3S" or "L2WW-0100-4S"
in trail-off wax., 1960.............................. **500.00 – 1,000.**

❑ RCA Victor 47-7777, black label, dog on top, with standard mix of "It's Now or Never", 1960.....................**10.00 - 20.00**

❑ RCA Victor 47-7777, picture sleeve, 1960 ....**30.00 - 60.00**

❑ RCA Victor 61-7777, "Living Stereo" on label, large hole, plays at 45 rpm, 1960 ....**200.00 - 400.00**

❑ RCA Victor 447-0628, black label, dog on top, 1962 **6.00 - 12.00**

❑ RCA Victor 447-0628, black label, dog on left, 1965 **5.00 - 10.00**

❑ RCA Victor 447-0628, orange label, 1969 ....**12.50 - 25.00**

❑ RCA Victor 447-0628, red label, 1970....................**4.00 - 8.00**

❑ RCA 447-0628, black label, dog near top, no "Victor" on label, 1977..**2.00 - 4.00**

❑ RCA PB-11110, from box "15 Golden Records, 30 Golden Hits," 1977...................................**2.00 - 4.00**

❑ RCA PB-11110, picture sleeve, 1977.....................**2.00 - 4.00**

❑ RCA Victor 47-7777, black label, dog on top, red vinyl, "DRE1 3045" in trail-off wax, from box "Elvis #1 Hit Singles Collection," 2001 ....**2.00 - 4.00**

❑ RCA Victor 47-7777, picture sleeve, "This is a replica of the
original packaging" on rear along bottom left,
2001..**2.00 - 4.00**

It's Now or Never/Surrender

❑ RCA PB-13889, from box "Elvis' Greatest Hits, Golden Singles,
Volume 1"; gold vinyl, 1984..............................**2.00 - 4.00**

❑ RCA PB-13889, picture sleeve, 1984......................**2.00 - 4.00**

It's Only Love/Beyond the Reef

❑ Collectables COL-4744, 1997..............................**1.00 - 3.00**

It's Only Love/The Sound of Your Cry

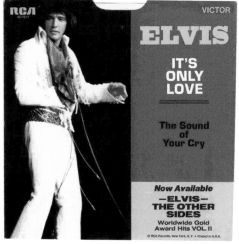

❑ RCA Victor 48-1017, orange label, 1971...............**3.00 - 6.00**

❑ RCA Victor 48-1017, yellow label promo, 1971......**15.00 - 30.00**

❑ RCA Victor 48-1017, picture sleeve, 1971 ....**7.50 - 15.00**

❑ RCA Victor 447-0684, red label, 1972..................**4.00 - 8.00**

❑ RCA 447-0684, black label, dog near top, no "Victor"
on label, 1977..**2.00 - 4.00**

Jailhouse Rock/Treat Me Nice

❑ RCA Victor 47-7035, East Coast pressing with horizontal
line on label, 1957.....................................**15.00 - 30.00**

❑ RCA Victor 47-7035, Midwest or West Coast pressing
without horizontal line on label, 1957 ....**15.00 - 30.00**

❑ RCA Victor 47-7035, gold label, dog on top;
gold vinyl, 1957......................................**7,500 – 10,000**

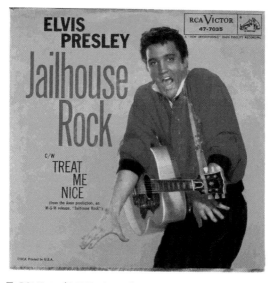

❏ RCA Victor 47-7035, picture sleeve, 1957 .... **50.00 - 100.00**

❏ RCA Victor 447-0619, black label, dog on top, 1959 **7.50 - 15.00**

❏ RCA Victor 447-0619, black label, dog on left, 1965 **5.00 - 10.00**

❏ RCA Victor 447-0619, orange label, 1969 .... **12.50 - 25.00**

❑ RCA Victor 447-0619, red label, 1970................**4.00 - 8.00**

❑ RCA 447-0619, black label, dog near top, no "Victor"
on label, 1977..**2.00 - 4.00**

❑ RCA PB-11101, from box "15 Golden Records,
30 Golden Hits," 1977..................................**2.00 - 4.00**

❑ RCA PB-11101, picture sleeve, 1977................**2.00 - 4.00**

❑ RCA Victor 47-7035, black label, dog on top, red vinyl,
"DRE1 3040" in trail-off wax, from box "Elvis #1 Hit
Singles Collection," 2001..............................**2.00 - 4.00**

❑ RCA Victor 47-7035, picture sleeve, "This is a replica of the
original packaging" on rear along lower right edge,
2001..**2.00 - 4.00**

Joshua Fit the Battle/Known Only to Him

❑ RCA Victor 447-0651, black label, dog on left, 1966 **7.50 - 15.00**

❑ RCA Victor 447-0651, white label promo, "Not for Sale"
on label, 1966...**60.00 - 120.00**

❑ RCA Victor 447-0651, picture sleeve, 1966....... **100.00 - 200.00**

❑ RCA Victor 447-0651, red label, 1970................**4.00 - 8.00**

❑ RCA 447-0651, black label, dog near top, no "Victor"
on label, 1977..**2.00 - 4.00**

Kentucky Rain/My Little Friend

❑ RCA Victor 47-9791, orange label, 1969................**4.00 - 8.00**

❑ RCA Victor 47-9791, yellow label promo, "Not for Sale"
on label, 1969...**15.00 - 30.00**

❑ RCA Victor 47-9791, picture sleeve, 1969 .... **7.50 - 15.00**

❑ RCA Victor 447-0675, red label, 1971....................**4.00 - 8.00**

❑ RCA 447-0675, black label, dog near top, no "Victor"
on label, 1977...**2.00 - 4.00**

❑ Collectables 80015, gray marbled vinyl, 1997.........**2.00 - 4.00**

❑ RCA Victor 47-9791, orange label, red vinyl, "DRE 13228"
    in trail-off wax, from box "Elvis Hit Singles Collection,
    Volume 2," 2002 ....**2.00 - 4.00**

❑ RCA Victor 47-9791, picture sleeve, "This is a replica of the
    original packaging" on rear along right edge, 2002 **2.00 - 4.00**

King of the Whole Wide World/
Home Is Where the Heart Is

❑ RCA Victor SP-45-118, black label, dog on top,
    "Not for Sale" on label, 1962....................**100.00 - 200.00**

❑ RCA Victor SP-45-118, picture sleeve, counterfeits
    exist but have red print; originals have black print,
    1962..**150.00 - 300.00**

King of the Whole Wide World/King Creole

❑ RCA DME1-1803, gold vinyl (about 7,000 pressed),
    1997...**4.00 - 8.00**

❑ RCA DME1-1803, test pressings on green, blue, white
    and clear vinyl; value is for any of them., 1997**200.00 - 400.00**

❑ RCA DME1-1803, picture sleeve, both 1803 and 1803R
    use the same sleeve, 1997 ....**4.00 - 8.00**

❑ RCA DME1-1803R, red vinyl, marked as a promotional
    copy (about 3,000 pressed), 1997....................**7.50 - 15.00**

Kiss Me Quick/Suspicion

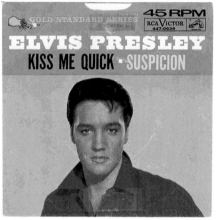

- ❏ RCA Victor 447-0639, black label, dog on top, 1964 **5.00 - 10.00**
- ❏ RCA Victor 447-0639, white label promo, "Not for Sale" on label, 1964 .... **25.00 - 50.00**
- ❏ RCA Victor 447-0639, picture sleeve, 1964 .... **20.00 - 40.00**
- ❏ RCA Victor 447-0639, orange label, 1969 .... **12.50 - 25.00**
- ❏ RCA Victor 447-0639, red label, 1970 .... **4.00 - 8.00**
- ❏ RCA 447-0639, black label, dog near top, no "Victor" on label, 1977 .... **2.00 - 4.00**
- ❏ Collectables 80016, gray marbled vinyl, 1997 .... **2.00 - 4.00**

Kissin' Cousins/It Hurts Me

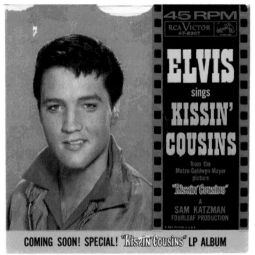

❑ RCA Victor 47-8307, black label, dog on top, 1964 .. **6.00 - 12.00**

❑ RCA Victor 47-8307, picture sleeve, 1964 .... **12.50 - 25.00**

❑ RCA Victor 447-0644, black label, dog on left, 1965 **5.00 - 10.00**

❑ RCA Victor 447-0644, orange label, 1969 .... **12.50 - 25.00**

❑ RCA Victor 447-0644, red label, 1970 .... **4.00 - 8.00**

❑ RCA 447-0644, black label, dog near top, no "Victor"
on label, 1977..**2.00 - 4.00**

❑ Collectables 80017, gray marbled vinyl, 1997..........**2.00 - 4.00**

Lawdy Miss Clawdy/Shake, Rattle, and Roll

"Picture sleeves" of RCA Victor 47-6642 are bootlegs.

❑ RCA Victor 47-6642, East Coast pressing with horizontal line
on label, dog on label as usual, 1956...............**20.00 - 40.00**

❑ RCA Victor 47-6642, East Coast pressing with horizontal line
on label, but with no dog, 1956.................. **100.00 - 200.00**

❑ RCA Victor 47-6642, Midwest or West Coast pressing
without horizontal line on label, 1956 ....**20.00 - 40.00**

❑ RCA Victor 447-0615, black label, dog on top, 1959 **7.50 - 15.00**

❑ RCA Victor 447-0615, black label, dog on left, 1965 **5.00 - 10.00**

❑ RCA Victor 447-0615, orange label, 1969............**12.50 - 25.00**

❑ RCA Victor 447-0615, red label, 1970...................**4.00 - 8.00**

❑ RCA 447-0615, black label, dog near top, no "Victor"
on label, 1977..**2.00 - 4.00**

Let Me Be There (mono/stereo)

❑ RCA JH-10951, light yellow label, promo only, "Not for Sale"
on label, 1977.................................... **100.00 - 200.00**

(Let Me Be Your) Teddy Bear/Loving You

❑ RCA Victor 47-7000, Label says "Let Me Be Your TEDDY BEAR"
(no parentheses), 1957 ....**20.00 - 40.00**

❑ RCA Victor 47-7000, Parentheses around "Let Me Be Your",
no horizontal line on label, 1957 ....**15.00 - 30.00**

❏ RCA Victor 47-7000, Parentheses around "Let Me Be Your",
with horizontal line on label, 1957 ....**15.00 - 30.00**

❏ RCA Victor 47-7000, picture sleeve, 1957 ....**60.00 - 120.00**

❏ RCA Victor 447-0620, black label, dog on top, 1959 **7.50 - 15.00**

❏ RCA Victor 447-0620, black label, dog on left, 1965 **5.00 - 10.00**

❏ RCA Victor 447-0620, orange label, 1969 ....**12.50 - 25.00**

❏ RCA Victor 447-0620, red label, 1970 ....**4.00 - 8.00**

❏ RCA 447-0620, black label, dog near top, 1977 ....**2.00 - 4.00**

❏ RCA PB-11109, from boxes "15 Golden Records,
30 Golden Hits" and "20 Golden Hits in Full
Color Sleeves," 1977 ....**2.00 - 4.00**

❏ RCA PB-11109, picture sleeve, 1977 ....**2.00 - 4.00**

❏ Collectables 80019, gray marbled vinyl, 1997 ....**2.00 - 4.00**

❏ RCA Victor 47-7000, parentheses around
"Let Me Be Your," black label, dog on top, red vinyl,
"DRE1 3039" in trail-off wax, from box "Elvis #1
Hit Singles Collection," 2001 ....**2.00 - 4.00**

❏ RCA Victor 47-7000, picture sleeve, "This is a replica
of the original packaging" on rear along
right edge, 2001 ....**2.00 - 4.00**

(Let Me Be Your) Teddy Bear/Puppet on a String

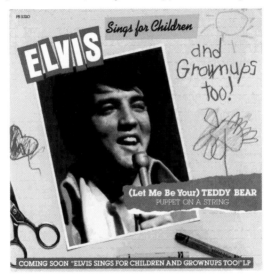

❏ RCA PB-11320, black label, dog near top, 1978........**2.50 - 5.00**

❏ RCA PB-11320, picture sleeve, 1978....................**5.00 - 10.00**

Let Yourself Go/Your Time Hasn't Come Yet, Baby

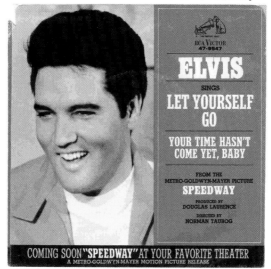

❑ RCA Victor 47-9547, black label, dog on left, 1968.. **5.00 - 10.00**

❑ RCA Victor 47-9547, yellow label promo, "Not for Sale"
on label, 1968..**30.00 - 60.00**

❑ RCA Victor 47-9547, picture sleeve, with *"Coming Soon –
Speedway LP"* on sleeve, 1968 ....**12.50 - 25.00**

❑ RCA Victor 47-9547, picture sleeve, with *"Ask For –*
   Speedway LP" on sleeve, 1968 ....**12.50 - 25.00**

❑ RCA Victor 447-0666, red label, 1970 ....**4.00 - 8.00**

❑ RCA 447-0666, black label, dog near top, no "Victor"
   on label, 1977 ....**2.00 - 4.00**

Life/Only Believe

❑ RCA Victor 47-9985, orange label, 1971 ....**3.00 - 6.00**

❑ RCA Victor 47-9985, picture sleeve, 1971 ....**15.00 - 30.00**

❑ RCA Victor 447-0682, red label, 1972 ....**2.50 - 8.00**

❑ RCA 447-0682, black label, dog near top, no "Victor"
   on label, 1977 ....**2.00 - 4.00**

A Little Less Conversation (JXL Radio Edit Remix)/ (Original Version)

❑ RCA 07863-60575-7, Credited to "Elvis Presley:
   Elvis vs JXL," 2002 ....**4.00 - 8.00**

A Little Less Conversation/Almost in Love

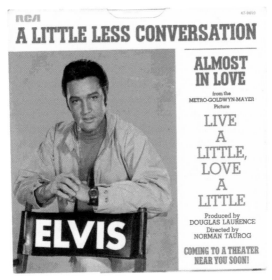

❑ RCA Victor 47-9610, black label, dog on left, 1968.. **5.00 - 10.00**

❑ RCA Victor 47-9610, yellow label promo, "Not for Sale"
   on label, 1968..**20.00 - 40.00**

❑ RCA Victor 47-9610, picture sleeve, 1968 ....**12.50 - 25.00**

❑ RCA Victor 447-0667, red label, 1970...................**4.00 - 8.00**

❑ RCA 447-0667, black label, dog near top, no "Victor"
on label, 1977 ....**2.00 - 4.00**

Little Sister/Paralyzed

❑ RCA JB-13547, promo only on blue vinyl, 1983. **150.00 - 300.00**

❑ RCA PB-13547, black label, dog near top, 1983.......**2.50 - 5.00**

❑ RCA PB-13547, picture sleeve, 1983...................**5.00 - 10.00**

LONELY MAN/SURRENDER

See SURRENDER/LONELY MAN.

**Long Legged Girl (With the Short Dress On)/
That's Someone You Never Forget**

❏ RCA Victor 47-9115, black label, dog on left, 1967 **5.00 - 10.00**

❏ RCA Victor 47-9115, white label promo, "Not for Sale"
on label, 1967 ....**20.00 - 40.00**

❑ RCA Victor 47-9115, picture sleeve, with *"Coming Soon – Double Trouble LP Album"* on sleeve, 1967.........**12.50 - 25.00**

❑ RCA Victor 47-9115, picture sleeve, with *"Ask For – Double Trouble LP Album"* on sleeve, 1967.........**15.00 - 30.00**

❑ RCA Victor 447-0660, red label, 1970................**20.00 - 40.00**

Love Letters/Come What May

❑ RCA Victor 47-8870, black label, dog on left, 1966.. **5.00 - 10.00**

❑ RCA Victor 47-8870, white label promo, "Not for Sale" on label, 1966.............................**25.00 - 50.00**

❑ RCA Victor 47-8870, picture sleeve, with *"Coming Soon – Paradise Hawaiian Style"* on sleeve, 1966...........**12.50 - 25.00**

❑ RCA Victor 47-8870, picture sleeve, with *"Ask For – Paradise Hawaiian Style"* on sleeve, 1966...........**25.00 - 50.00**

❑ RCA Victor 447-0657, black label, dog on left, 1968 **5.00 - 10.00**

❑ RCA Victor 447-0657, red label, 1970...................**4.00 - 8.00**

❑ RCA 447-0657, black label, dog near top, no "Victor" on label, 1977...**2.00 - 4.00**

**Love Me Tender/Any way You Want Me
(That's How I Will Be)**

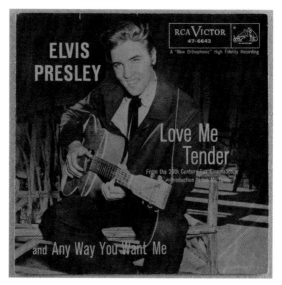

❑ RCA Victor 47-6643, East Coast pressing with horizontal
line on label, "From the 20th-Century Fox CinemaScope
Production 'Love Me Tender'" under the A-side song title,
1956..**15.00 - 30.00**

❏ RCA Victor 47-6643, East Coast pressing with horizontal line on label, no reference to the movie "Love Me Tender" on A-side label, 1956 ....**20.00 - 40.00**

❏ RCA Victor 47-6643, Midwest or West Coast pressing without horizontal line on label, 1956 ....**15.00 - 30.00**

❏ RCA Victor 47-6643, picture sleeve, black and light pink sleeve, 1956.......................................**15.00 - 30.00**

❏ RCA Victor 47-6643, picture sleeve, black and dark pink sleeve, 1956.......................................**20.00 - 40.00**

❏ RCA Victor 47-6643, picture sleeve, black and green sleeve, 1956..**37.50 - 75.00**

❏ RCA Victor 47-6643, picture sleeve, black and white sleeve, 1956..**90.00 - 180.00**

❏ RCA Victor 447-0616, black label, dog on top, 1959 **7.50 - 15.00**

❏ RCA Victor 447-0616, black label, dog on left, 1965 **5.00 - 10.00**

❏ RCA Victor 447-0616, orange label, 1969 ....**12.50 - 25.00**

❏ RCA Victor 447-0616, red label, 1970...................**4.00 - 8.00**

❏ RCA 447-0616, black label, dog near top, no "Victor" on label, 1977..**2.00 - 4.00**

❏ RCA PB-11108, from boxes "15 Golden Records, 30 Golden Hits" and "20 Golden Hits in Full Color Sleeves," 1977....**2.00 - 4.00**

❏ RCA PB-11108, picture sleeve, 1977.......................**2.00 - 4.00**

❏ RCA Victor 47-6643, black label, dog on top, red vinyl, "DRE1-3036" in trail-off wax, from box "Elvis #1 Hit Singles Collection," 2001 ....**2.00 - 4.00**

❏ RCA Victor 47-6643, picture sleeve, black and light pink version, "This is a replica of the original packaging" on rear along bottom, 2001 ....**2.00 - 4.00**

Love Me Tender/Loving You

❏ RCA PB-13893, From box "Elvis' Greatest Hits, Golden Singles, Volume 2"; gold vinyl, 1984 ....**2.00 - 4.00**

❏ RCA PB-13893, picture sleeve, 1984 ....**2.00 - 4.00**

Love Me/Flaming Star

❏ Collectables COL-4514, black vinyl, 1986 ....**1.00 - 3.00**

❏ Collectables COL-4514, gold vinyl, 1992 ....**2.00 - 4.00**

Lovin' Arms/You Asked Me To

"Picture sleeves" of RCA JB- or PB-12205 are bootlegs.

❏ RCA JB-12205, yellow label promo, green vinyl, 1981 ....**150.00 - 300.00**

❏ RCA JB-12205, yellow label promo, black vinyl, 1981 ....**7.50 - 15.00**

❏ RCA PB-12205, black label, dog near top, 1981 ....**3.00 - 6.00**

(Marie's the Name) His Latest Flame/Little Sister

Most, if not all, variations of this record list the title of the A-side as "Marie's the Name HIS LATEST FLAME," with no parentheses.

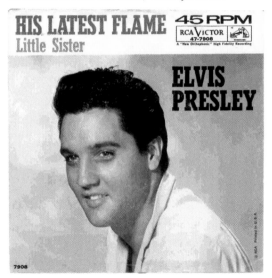

❑ RCA Victor 37-7908, "Compact Single 33" (small hole, plays at LP speed), 1961 .... **750.00 – 1,500.**

❑ RCA Victor 37-7908, picture sleeve, must have "Compact 33 Single" and "37-7880" on sleeve, with "New Orthophonic" under RCA Victor box at upper right, 1961........**1,500 – 2,000**

❑ RCA Victor 37-7908, picture sleeve, must have "Compact 33 Single" and "37-7880" on sleeve, with "Stereo-Orthophonic" under RCA Victor box at right, 1961.............**2,000 – 2,500**

❑ RCA Victor 47-7908, black label, dog on top, 1961.**10.00 - 20.00**

❑ RCA Victor 47-7908, picture sleeve, 1961 ....**25.00 - 50.00**

❑ RCA Victor 447-0634, black label, dog on top, 1962 **6.00 - 12.00**

❑ RCA Victor 447-0634, black label, dog on left, 1965 **5.00 - 10.00**

❑ RCA Victor 447-0634, orange label, 1969...........**12.50 - 25.00**

❑ RCA Victor 447-0634, red label, 1970.................**4.00 - 8.00**

❑ RCA 447-0634, black label, dog near top, no "Victor" on label, 1977 ....**2.00 - 4.00**

❑ RCA PB-13894, from box "Elvis' Greatest Hits, Golden Singles, Volume 2"; gold vinyl, 1984 ....**2.00 - 4.00**

❑ RCA PB-13894, picture sleeve, 1984.....................**2.00 - 4.00**

❑ Collectables 80018, gray marbled vinyl, 1997..........**2.00 - 4.00**

❑ RCA Victor 47-7908, black label, dog on top, red vinyl, "DRE 13226" in trail-off wax, from box "Elvis Hit Singles Collection, Volume 2," 2002.................**2.00 - 4.00**

❑ RCA Victor 47-7908, picture sleeve, "This is a replica of the original packaging" on rear along lower right edge, 2002 ....**2.00 - 4.00**

Memories/Charro

❑ RCA Victor 47-9731, orange label, 1969................**4.00 - 8.00**

❑ RCA Victor 47-9731, yellow label promo, "Not for Sale" on label, 1969.......................................**15.00 - 30.00**

❑ RCA Victor 47-9731, picture sleeve, 1969 ....**10.00 - 20.00**

❑ RCA Victor 447-0669, red label, 1970...................**4.00 - 8.00**

❑ RCA 447-0669, black label, dog near top, no "Victor" on label, 1977...**2.00 - 4.00**

❑ Collectables 80021, gray marbled vinyl, 1997.........**2.00 - 4.00**

Merry Christmas Baby/O Come All Ye Faithful

❑ RCA Victor 74-0572, orange label, 1971...............**7.50 - 15.00**

❑ RCA Victor 74-0572, yellow label promo, "Not for Sale" on label, 1971...**15.00 - 30.00**

❑ RCA Victor 74-0572, picture sleeve, 1971 ....**20.00 - 40.00**

Merry Christmas Baby/Santa Claus Is Back in Town

❑ RCA PB-14237, "Elvis 50th Anniversary" label,
  black vinyl, 1985..**7.50 - 15.00**

❑ RCA PB-14237, "Elvis 50th Anniversary" label,
  green vinyl, 1985 ....**7.50 - 15.00**

❑ RCA PB-14237, black label, dog near top, 1985........**2.50 - 5.00**

❑ RCA PB-14237, picture sleeve, 1985....................**6.00 - 12.00**

Milkcow Blues Boogie/You're a Heartbreaker

Other than the 2001 sleeve listed, "picture sleeves" of Sun 215 and RCA Victor 47-6382 are bootlegs.

❏ Sun 215, 1955 (beware of counterfeits)............**3,000 – 5,000**

❏ RCA Victor 47-6382, East Coast pressing with horizontal line on label, 1955...**30.00 - 60.00**

❏ RCA Victor 47-6382, Midwest or West Coast pressing without horizontal line on label, 1955.......................**30.00 - 60.00**

❏ RCA Victor 447-0603, black label, dog on top, 1959 **7.50 - 15.00**

❑ RCA Victor 447-0603, black label, dog on left, 1965 **5.00 - 10.00**

❑ RCA Victor 447-0603, orange label, 1969 ....**12.50 - 25.00**

❑ RCA Victor 447-0603, red label, 1970 ....**4.00 - 8.00**

❑ RCA 447-0603, black label, dog near top, no "Victor"
on label, 1977 ....**2.00 - 4.00**

❑ Collectables COL-4501, black vinyl, 1986 ....**1.00 - 3.00**

❑ Collectables COL-4501, gold vinyl, 1992 ....**2.00 - 4.00**

❑ Sun 215, red vinyl, "DRE-13053" in trail-off wax, from box
"Elvis #1 Hit Singles Collection," 2001 ....**2.00 - 4.00**

❑ Sun 215, picture sleeve, "Sun ® Records is a registered
trademark" on rear along lower left edge, 2001 .....**2.00 - 4.00**

Milky White Way/Swing Down Sweet Chariot

❑ RCA Victor 447-0652, black label, dog on left, 1966 **7.50 - 15.00**

❑ RCA Victor 447-0652, white label promo, "Not for Sale"
on label, 1966 ....**60.00 - 120.00**

❑ RCA Victor 447-0652, picture sleeve, 1966 ....**100.00 - 200.00**

❑ RCA Victor 447-0652, red label, 1970 ....**4.00 - 8.00**

Money Honey/One-Sided Love Affair

"Picture sleeves" of RCA Victor 47-6641 are bootlegs.

❑ RCA Victor 47-6641, East Coast pressing
   with horizontal line on label, 1956 ....**25.00 - 50.00**

❑ RCA Victor 47-6641, Midwest or West Coast pressing
   without horizontal line on label, 1956 ....**25.00 - 50.00**

❑ RCA Victor 447-0614, black label, dog on top, 1959 **7.50 - 15.00**

❑ RCA Victor 447-0614, black label, dog on left, 1965 **5.00 - 10.00**

❑ RCA Victor 447-0614, orange label, 1969 ....**12.50 - 25.00**

❑ RCA Victor 447-0614, red label, 1970...................**4.00 - 8.00**

❑ RCA 447-0614, black label, dog near top, no "Victor"
   on label, 1977 ....**2.00 - 4.00**

❑ Collectables COL-4506, black vinyl, 1986..............**1.00 - 3.00**

❑ Collectables COL-4506, gold vinyl, 1992 ....**2.00 - 4.00**

Moody Blue/For the Heart

❑ RCA GB-11326, black label, dog near top, 1978 ....**2.00 - 4.00**

Moody Blue/She Thinks I Still Care

❏ RCA JB-10857, light yellow label, "Not for Sale"
   on label, 1976 .... **7.50 - 15.00**

❏ RCA PB-10857, black label, dog near top, 1976 .... **2.50 - 5.00**

❏ RCA PB-10857, black label, dog near top,
experimental colored vinyl pressing; five different
colors exist – red, white, gold, blue, and green;
value is for any one of them., 1976 ....**1,500 – 2,000**

❏ RCA PB-10857, picture sleeve, 1976 ....**5.00 - 10.00**

My Boy (MOno/stereo)

❏ RCA Victor JH-10191, light yellow label promo,
"Not for Sale" on label, 1975 ....**15.00 - 30.00**

My Boy/LOVING ARMS

❏ RCA Victor RCA-2458EX, gray label, printed in U.S.
for export, 1975 ....**250.00 - 500.00**

❏ RCA Victor RCA-2458EX, paper insert, white with
green and black print, 1975 ....**100.00 - 200.00**

My Boy/Thinking About You

❑ RCA Victor PB-10191, orange label, 1975..............**2.50 - 5.00**

❑ RCA Victor PB-10191, tan label, 1975 ....**2.50 - 5.00**

❑ RCA Victor PB-10191, picture sleeve, 1975............**5.00 - 10.00**

❑ RCA Victor GB-10489, red label, 1975 ....**4.00 - 8.00**

❑ RCA GB-10489, black label, dog near top, no "Victor" on label, 1977 ....**2.00 - 4.00**

❑ Collectables 80022, gray marbled vinyl, 1997.........**2.00 - 4.00**

My Way/America

❑ RCA JH-11165, light yellow label promo, "Not for Sale" on label, 1977 ....**10.00 - 20.00**

❑ RCA PB-11165, black label, dog near top, 1977........**2.50 - 5.00**

❑ RCA PB-11165, picture sleeve, 1977...................**5.00 - 10.00**

My Way/America the Beautiful

❑ RCA PB-11165, black label, dog near top, 1977.....**10.00 - 20.00**

❑ RCA PB-11165, picture sleeve, 1977..................**12.50 - 25.00**

Mystery Train/I Forgot to Remember to Forget

See I FORGOT TO REMEMBER TO FORGET/MYSTERY TRAIN.

(Now and Then There's) A Fool Such As I/I Need Your Love Tonight

❑ RCA Victor 47-7506, black label, dog near top,
1959..**12.50 - 25.00**

❑ RCA Victor 47-7506, picture sleeve, lists Elvis' EPs
and Gold Standard singles on back, 1959.........**30.00 - 60.00**

❑ RCA Victor 47-7506, picture sleeve, promotes the
"Elvis Sails" EP on back, 1959 .... **500.00 – 1,000.**

❑ RCA Victor 447-0625, black label, dog on top, 1961 **7.50 - 15.00**

❑ RCA Victor 447-0625, black label, dog on left, 1965 **5.00 - 10.00**

❑ RCA Victor 447-0625, orange label, 1969...........**12.50 - 25.00**

❑ RCA Victor 447-0625, red label, 1970....................**4.00 - 8.00**

❑ RCA 447-0625, black label, dog near top, no "Victor"
on label, 1977...**2.00 - 4.00**

❑ Collectables 80000, gray marbled vinyl, 1997..........**2.00 - 4.00**

❑ RCA Victor 47-7506, black label, dog near top, red vinyl,
"DRE 13220" in trail-off wax, from box "Elvis Hit Singles
Collection, Volume 2," 2002 ....**2.00 - 4.00**

❑ RCA Victor 47-7506, picture sleeve, lists Elvis' EPs and
Gold Standard singles on back, "This is a replica of the original
packaging" on rear along lower right edge, 2002 ...**2.00 - 4.00**

Old Shep (b-side blank)

❑ RCA Victor CR-15, white label promo, authentic copes
have the trail-off number machine-starmped in the
dead wax, 1956.....................................**500.00 – 1,000.**

Old Shep/You'll Never Walk Alone

❑ Collectables COL-4518, black vinyl, 1986...............**1.00 - 3.00**

❑ Collectables COL-4518, gold vinyl, 1992 ....**2.00 - 4.00**

One Broken Heart for Sale/
(you're the) Devil in Disguise

❑ Collectables COL-4512, black vinyl, 1986...............**1.00 - 3.00**

❑ Collectables COL-4512, gold vinyl, 1992 ....**2.00 - 4.00**

One Broken Heart for Sale/
They Remind Me Too Much of You

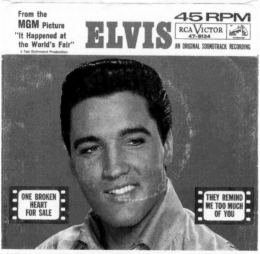

❏ RCA Victor 47-8134, black label, dog on top, 1963 .. **6.00 - 12.00**

❏ RCA Victor 47-8134, picture sleeve, 1963 ....**15.00 - 30.00**

❏ RCA Victor 447-0640, black label, dog on top,
   1964..**12.50 - 25.00**

❏ RCA Victor 447-0640, black label,
   dog on left, 1965..................................**5.00 - 10.00**

❏ RCA Victor 447-0640, orange label, 1969...........**12.50 - 25.00**

❏ RCA Victor 447-0640, red label, 1970..................**4.00 - 8.00**

❏ RCA 447-0640, black label, dog near top,
   no "Victor" on label, 1977..............................**2.00 - 4.00**

❏ RCA Victor 47-8134, black label, dog on top, red vinyl,
   "DRE 13219" in trail-off wax, from box
   "Elvis Hit Singles Collection, Volume 2," 2002......**2.00 - 4.00**

❏ RCA Victor 47-8134, picture sleeve, "This is a
   replica of the original packaging" on rear
   along right edge, 2002....................................**2.00 - 4.00**

One Night/I Got Stung

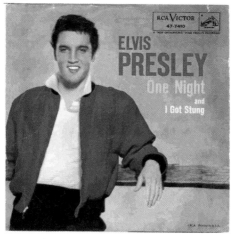

- ❑ RCA Victor 47-7410, black label, dog on top, 1958 **12.50 - 25.00**
- ❑ RCA Victor 47-7410, picture sleeve, 1958 ....**35.00 - 70.00**
- ❑ RCA Victor 447-0624, black label, dog on top, 1961 **6.00 - 12.00**
- ❑ RCA Victor 447-0624, black label, dog on left, 1965..**5.00 - 10.00**
- ❑ RCA Victor 447-0624, orange label, 1969 ....**12.50 - 25.00**
- ❑ RCA Victor 447-0624, red label, 1970....................**4.00 - 8.00**

❑ RCA 447-0624, black label, dog near top,
no "Victor" on label, 1977 ....**2.00 - 4.00**

❑ RCA PB-11112, from box "15 Golden Records,
30 Golden Hits," 1977....................................**2.00 - 4.00**

❑ RCA PB-11112, picture sleeve, 1977.....................**2.00 - 4.00**

❑ Collectables 80011, gray marbled vinyl, 1997..........**2.00 - 4.00**

❑ RCA Victor 47-7410, black label, dog on top, red vinyl,
"DRE 13237" in trail-off wax, from box "Elvis Hit Singles
Collection, Volume 2," 2002 ....**2.00 - 4.00**

❑ RCA Victor 47-7410, picture sleeve, "This is a replica of the
original packaging" on rear at lower right, 2002....**2.00 - 4.00**

Patch It Up/You Don't Have to Say You Love Me

See YOU DON'T HAVE TO SAY YOU LOVE ME/PATCH IT UP.

Playing for Keeps/Too much

See TOO MUCH/PLAYING FOR KEEPS.

Poor Boy/An American Trilogy

❑ Collectables COL-4519, black vinyl, 1986...............**1.00 - 3.00**

❑ Collectables COL-4519, gold vinyl, 1992 ....**2.00 - 4.00**

Promised Land/It's Midnight

❑ RCA Victor PB-10074, gray label, 1974 ....**2.50 - 5.00**

❑ RCA Victor PB-10074, orange label, 1974 ....**2.50 - 5.00**

❑ RCA Victor PB-10074, picture sleeve, 1974 ....**5.00 - 10.00**

❑ RCA Victor PB-10074, tan label, 1975 ....**12.50 - 25.00**

❑ RCA Victor GB-10488, red label, 1975 ....**4.00 - 8.00**

❑ RCA GB-10488, black label, dog near top, no "Victor"
    on label, 1977 ....**2.00 - 4.00**

Puppet on a String/Wooden Heart

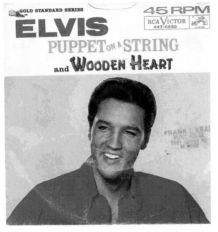

- ❑ RCA Victor 447-0650, black label, dog on left, 1965 **5.00 - 10.00**
- ❑ RCA Victor 447-0650, white label promo,
  "Not for Sale" on label, 1965.........................**15.00 - 30.00**
- ❑ RCA Victor 447-0650, picture sleeve, 1965...........**15.00 - 30.00**
- ❑ RCA Victor 447-0650, red label, 1970....................**4.00 - 8.00**
- ❑ RCA 447-0650, black label, dog near top, no
  "Victor" on label, 1977 ....**2.00 - 4.00**
- ❑ Collectables 80028, gray marbled vinyl, 1997..........**2.00 - 4.00**

Raised on Rock/For Ol' Times Sake

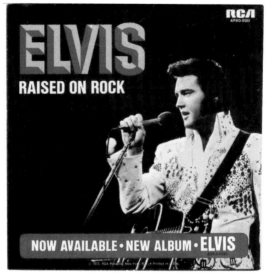

❏ RCA Victor APBO-0088, orange label, 1973............**3.00 - 6.00**

❏ RCA Victor APBO-0088, picture sleeve, 1973..........**7.50 - 15.00**

❏ RCA Victor DJAO-0088, light yellow label promo,
   "Not for Sale" on label, 1973......................**10.00 - 20.00**

Raised on Rock/If You Talk in Your Sleep

❏ RCA Victor GB-10157,red label, 1975 .... **4.00 - 8.00**

❏ RCA GB-10157, black label, dog near top, no "Victor"
on label, 1977 .... **2.00 - 4.00**

Return to Sender/Where Do You Come From

❏ RCA Victor 47-8100, black label, dog on top, 1962 **10.00 - 20.00**

❏ RCA Victor 47-8100, picture sleeve, 1962 .... **20.00 - 40.00**

❑ RCA Victor 447-0638, black label, dog on top, 1963 **6.00 - 12.00**

❑ RCA Victor 447-0638, black label, dog on left, 1965 **5.00 - 10.00**

❑ RCA Victor 447-0638, orange label, 1969 .... **12.50 - 25.00**

❑ RCA Victor 447-0638, red label, 1970 .... **4.00 - 8.00**

❑ RCA 447-0638, black label, dog near top, no "Victor"
on label, 1977 .... **2.00 - 4.00**

❑ RCA PB-11111, from boxes "15 Golden Records, 30 Golden Hits"
and "20 Golden Hits in Full Color Sleeves," 1977 .... **2.00 - 4.00**

❑ RCA PB-11111, picture sleeve, 1977 .... **2.00 - 4.00**

❑ RCA 47-8100, black label, dog near top, no "Victor" on label,
red vinyl, "DRE 13223" in trail-off wax, from box
"Elvis Hit Singles Collection, Volume 2," 2002 ...... **2.00 - 4.00**

❑ RCA Victor 47-8100, picture sleeve, "This is a replica of the
original packaging" on rear at lower left, 2002 ...... **2.00 - 4.00**

Roustabout/One Track Heart

❑ RCA Victor SP-45-139, white label, promo only,
"Not for Sale" on label, 1964 .... **150.00 - 300.00**

Rubberneckin' (Paul Oakenfold Remix Radio Edit)/ (Original)

❑ BMG 82876-56193-7, white label, 2003 .... **2.50 - 5.00**

Separate Ways/Always on My Mind

❏ RCA Victor 74-0815, orange label, 1972..............**3.00 - 6.00**

❏ RCA Victor 74-0815, yellow label promo,
"Not for Sale" on label, 1972......................**12.50 - 25.00**

❏ RCA Victor 74-0815, picture sleeve, 1972 ....**7.50 - 15.00**

❑ RCA Victor GB-10486, red label, 1975 .... **4.00 - 8.00**

❑ RCA GB-10486, black label, dog near top, no "Victor" on label, 1977 .... **2.00 - 4.00**

❑ Collectables 80001, gray marbled vinyl, 1997 .... **2.00 - 4.00**

She's Not You/Jailhouse Rock

❑ Collectables COL-4511, black vinyl, 1986 .... **1.00 - 3.00**

❑ Collectables COL-4511, gold vinyl, 1992 .... **2.00 - 4.00**

She's Not You/Just Tell Her Jim Said Hello

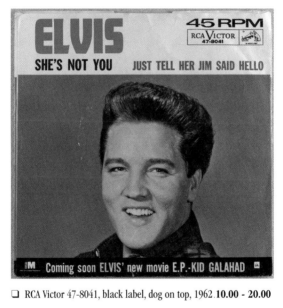

❑ RCA Victor 47-8041, black label, dog on top, 1962.**10.00 - 20.00**

❑ RCA Victor 47-8041, picture sleeve, 1962............**20.00 - 40.00**

❑ RCA Victor 447-0637, black label, dog on top, 1963 **6.00 - 12.00**

❑ RCA Victor 447-0637, black label, dog on left, 1965 **5.00 - 10.00**

❑ RCA Victor 447-0637, orange label, 1969 ....**12.50 - 25.00**

❑ RCA Victor 447-0637, red label, 1970 ....**4.00 - 8.00**

❑ RCA 447-0637, black label, dog near top, no "Victor"
on label, 1977 ....**2.00 - 4.00**

❑ RCA 47-8041, black label, dog near top, no "Victor" on label,
red vinyl, "DRE 13240" in trail-off wax, from box "Elvis Hit
Singles Collection, Volume 2," 2002 ....**2.00 - 4.00**

❑ RCA Victor 47-8041, picture sleeve, "This is a
replica of the original packaging" on rear along
lower right edge, 2002 ....**2.00 - 4.00**

Silver Bells (Unreleased Version)/Silver Bells

❑ RCA 62411-7, silver label, 1993 ....**2.50 - 5.00**

Spinout/All That I Am

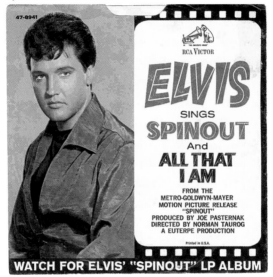

❑ RCA Victor 47-8941, black label, dog on left, 1966.. **5.00 - 10.00**

❑ RCA Victor 47-8941, white label promo, "Not for Sale"
on label, 1966...**25.00 - 50.00**

❑ RCA Victor 47-8941, picture sleeve, *"Watch For Elvis'*
Spinout LP" on sleeve, 1966..............................**12.50 - 25.00**

❑ RCA Victor 47-8941, picture sleeve,
"Ask For Elvis' Spinout LP"
on sleeve, 1966...**12.50 - 25.00**

❑ RCA Victor 447-0658, black label, dog on left,
1968...**5.00 - 10.00**

❑ RCA Victor 447-0658, red label, 1970...................**4.00 - 8.00**

❑ RCA 447-0658, black label, dog near top, no
"Victor" on label, 1977 ....**2.00 - 4.00**

Steamroller Blues/Fool

❑ RCA Victor 74-0910, orange label, 1973................**3.00 - 6.00**

❑ RCA Victor 74-0910, light yellow label promo,
"Not for Sale" on label, 1973............................**7.50 - 15.00**

❑ RCA Victor 74-0910, picture sleeve, 1973 ....**7.50 - 15.00**

Stuck on You/Fame and Fortune

❏ RCA Victor 47-7740, black label, dog on top, 1960.**10.00 - 20.00**

❏ RCA Victor 47-7740, picture sleeve, large hole in middle,
  has no titles on it but states, "Elvis' 1st New Recording
  for His 50,000,000 Fans All Around the World" at lower left,
  1960..**30.00 - 60.00**

❑ RCA Victor 61-7740, "Living Stereo" on label; large hole,
plays at 45 rpm, 1960............................**200.00 - 400.00**

❑ RCA Victor 447-0627, black label, dog on top,
1962..**6.00 - 12.00**

❑ RCA Victor 447-0627, black label, dog on left,
1965..**5.00 - 10.00**

❑ RCA Victor 447-0627, orange label, 1969............**12.50 - 25.00**

❑ RCA Victor 447-0627, red label, 1970....................**4.00 - 8.00**

❑ RCA 447-0627, black label, dog near top, no "Victor"
on label, 1977..**2.00 - 4.00**

❑ Collectables COL-4509, black vinyl, 1986..............**1.00 - 3.00**

❑ Collectables COL-4509, gold vinyl, 1992 ....**2.00 - 4.00**

❑ RCA Victor 47-7740, black label, dog on top, red vinyl,
"DRE1-3044" in trail-off wax, from box "Elvis #1
Hit Singles Collection," 2001 ....**2.00 - 4.00**

❑ RCA Victor 47-7740, picture sleeve, "This is a replica
of the original packaging" on rear along bottom
left edge, 2001..**2.00 - 4.00**

Such a Night/Never Ending

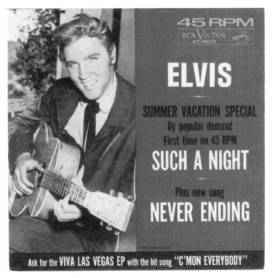

❑ RCA Victor 47-8400, black label, dog on top, 1964.. **6.00 - 12.00**

❑ RCA Victor 47-8400, white label, promo, "Not for Sale"
  on label, 1964 . . . . **3,500 – 5,000**

❑ RCA Victor 47-8400, picture sleeve, 1964 . . . . **12.50 - 25.00**

❏ RCA Victor 447-0645, black label, dog on top, 1965**20.00 - 40.00**

❏ RCA Victor 447-0645, black label, dog on left, 1965 **5.00 - 10.00**

❏ RCA Victor 447-0645, orange label, 1969 ....**12.50 - 25.00**

❏ RCA Victor 447-0645, red label, 1970 ....**4.00 - 8.00**

❏ RCA 447-0645, black label, dog near top, no "Victor"
on label, 1977 ....**2.00 - 4.00**

(Such An) Easy Question/It Feels So Right

❏ RCA Victor 47-8585, black label, dog on left, 1965 .. **5.00 - 10.00**

❏ RCA Victor 47-8585, white label promo, "Not for Sale"
on label, 1965 ....**25.00 - 50.00**

❏ RCA Victor 47-8585, picture sleeve, with *"Coming Soon!*
Special Tickle Me EP" on sleeve, 1965 ....**12.50 - 25.00**

❏ RCA Victor 47-8585, picture sleeve, with *"Ask For Special*
Tickle Me EP" on sleeve, 1965 ....**12.50 - 25.00**

❏ RCA Victor 447-0653, black label, dog on left, 1966 **5.00 - 10.00**

❏ RCA Victor 447-0653, red label, 1970 ....**4.00 - 8.00**

❏ RCA 447-0653, black label, dog near top, no "Victor"
on label, 1977 ....**2.00 - 4.00**

Surrender/Lonely Man

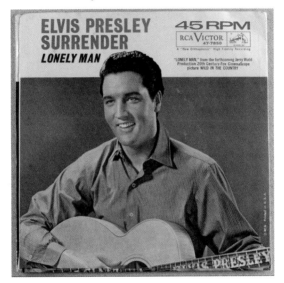

❑ RCA Victor 37-7850, "Compact Single 33"
(small hole, plays at LP speed), 1961 .... **300.00 - 600.00**

❑ RCA Victor 37-7850, picture sleeve, must have "Compact
33 Single" and "37-7850" on sleeve, 1961 ...... **500.00 – 1,000**

❑ RCA Victor 47-7850, black label, dog on top, 1961 **10.00 - 20.00**

❑ RCA Victor 47-7850, picture sleeve, 1961 ....**30.00 - 60.00**

❑ RCA Victor 61-7850, "Living Stereo" edition, large hole,
   plays at 45 rpm, 1961............................**400.00 - 800.00**

❑ RCA Victor 68-7850, "Compact Single 33"
   (small hole, plays at LP speed), but with "Living Stereo"
   on label, 1961.....................................**1,500 – 2,000**

❑ RCA Victor 447-0630, black label, dog on top, 1962 **12.50 - 25.00**

❑ RCA Victor 447-0630, black label, dog on left, 1965 **5.00 - 10.00**

❑ RCA Victor 447-0630, orange label, 1969 ....**12.50 - 25.00**

❑ RCA Victor 447-0630, red label, 1970..................**4.00 - 8.00**

❑ RCA 447-0630, black label, dog near top, no "Victor"
   on label, 1977.......................................**2.00 - 4.00**

❑ Collectables 80025, gray marbled vinyl, 1997..........**2.00 - 4.00**

❑ RCA Victor 47-7850, black label, dog on top, red vinyl,
   "DRE1 3047" in trail-off wax, from box "Elvis #1
   Hit Singles Collection," 2001 ....**2.00 - 4.00**

❑ RCA Victor 47-7850, picture sleeve, "This is a replica
   of the original packaging" on rear along lower
   right edge, 2001......................................**2.00 - 4.00**

Suspicious Minds/Burning Love

❑ RCA PB-13896, from box "Elvis' Greatest Hits, Golden
Singles, Volume 2"; gold vinyl, 1984 .... **2.00 - 4.00**

❑ RCA PB-13896, picture sleeve, 1984 .... **2.00 - 4.00**

Suspicious Minds/You'll Think of Me

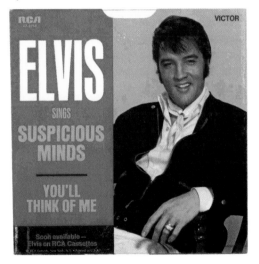

- ❏ RCA Victor 47-9764, orange label, 1969.................**4.00 - 8.00**

- ❏ RCA Victor 47-9764, yellow label promo,
  "Not for Sale" on label, 1969.................**15.00 - 30.00**

- ❏ RCA Victor 47-9764, picture sleeve, 1969 ....**10.00 - 20.00**

- ❏ RCA Victor 447-0673, red label, 1970..................**4.00 - 8.00**

- ❏ RCA 447-0673, black label, dog near top, no "Victor"
  on label, 1977................**2.00 - 4.00**

- ❏ RCA PB-11103, from box "15 Golden Records,
  30 Golden Hits," 1977................**2.00 - 4.00**

- ❏ RCA PB-11103, picture sleeve, 1977................**2.00 - 4.00**

- ❏ RCA GB-13275, black label, dog near top, 1982 ......**2.00 - 4.00**

- ❏ RCA Victor 47-9764, orange label, red vinyl,
  "DRE1-3050" in trail-off wax, from box "Elvis #1
  Hit Singles Collection," 2001 ....**2.00 - 4.00**

- ❏ RCA Victor 47-9764, picture sleeve, "This is a replica
  of the original packaging" on rear along lower right
  edge, 2001................**2.00 - 4.00**

T-R-O-U-B-L-E (MONO/STEREO)

- ❏ RCA Victor JH-10278, light yellow label promo,
  "Not for Sale" on label, 1975................**15.00 - 30.00**

T-R-O-U-B-L-E/Mr. Songman

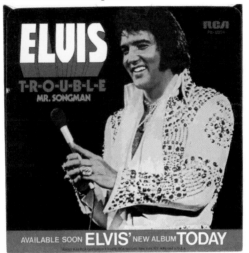

☐ RCA Victor PB-10278, gray label, 1975 .... **50.00 - 100.00**

☐ RCA Victor PB-10278, tan label, 1975 .... **5.00 - 10.00**

☐ RCA Victor PB-10278, orange label, 1975 .... **2.50 - 5.00**

☐ RCA Victor PB-10278, picture sleeve, 1975 .... **5.00 - 10.00**

❑ RCA Victor GB-10487, red label, 1975 ....**4.00 - 8.00**

❑ RCA GB-10487,black label, dog near top, no "Victor"
  on label, 1977 ....**2.00 - 4.00**

Take Good Care of Her/
I've Got a Thing About You, Baby

❑ RCA Victor APBO-0196, orange label, 1973............**3.00 - 6.00**

❑ RCA Victor APBO-0196, picture sleeve, 1973.......... **7.50 - 15.00**

❑ RCA Victor DJBO-0196, light yellow label, "Not for Sale"
  on label, 1973 ....**12.50 - 25.00**

❑ RCA Victor GB-10485, red label, 1975 ....**4.00 - 8.00**

❑ RCA GB-10485, black label, dog near top, no "Victor"
  on label, 1977 ....**2.00 - 4.00**

Teddy Bear/Loving You

See (LET ME BE YOUR) TEDDY BEAR/LOVING YOU.

Teddy Bear/Puppet on a String

See (LET ME BE YOUR) TEDDY BEAR/PUPPET ON A STRING.

Tell Me Pretty Baby (same on both sides)

Though credited to "Elvis Presley" with claims that it was his first professional recording, this record was actually by an impersonator.

❑ Cin Kay 064, 1978..**1.00 - 2.50**

❑ Cin Kay 064, picture sleeve, 1978.........................**1.00 - 2.50**

❑ Elvis Classic EC-5478, 1978 ....**1.00 - 2.50**

❑ Elvis Classic EC-5478, picture sleeve, 1978.............**1.00 - 2.50**

Tell Me Why/Blue River

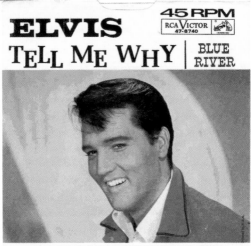

❏ RCA Victor 47-8740, black label, dog on left, 1965..**5.00 - 10.00**

❏ RCA Victor 47-8740, white label promo, "Not for Sale"
   on label, 1965..**25.00 - 50.00**

❏ RCA Victor 47-8740, picture sleeve, 1965 ....**12.50 - 25.00**

❏ RCA Victor 447-0655, black label, dog on left, 1968 **5.00 - 10.00**

❑ RCA Victor 447-0655, red label, 1970.....................**4.00 - 8.00**

❑ RCA 447-0655, black label, dog near top, no "Victor"
on label, 1977 ....**2.00 - 4.00**

That's All Right/Blue Moon of Kentucky

Other than the 2001 sleeve listed, "picture sleeves" of Sun 209 and RCA
Victor 47-6380 are bootlegs.

- ❏ Sun 209, 1954 (beware of counterfeits)..........**4,000 – 6,000 +**
- ❏ RCA Victor 47-6380, East Coast pressing with horizontal line on label, 1955....................**30.00 - 60.00**
- ❏ RCA Victor 47-6380, Midwest or West Coast pressing without horizontal line on label, 1955 ....**30.00 - 60.00**
- ❏ RCA Victor 447-0601, black label, dog on top, 1959 **7.50 - 15.00**
- ❏ RCA Victor 447-0601, white label promo, "Not for Sale" on label, 1964.....................**50.00 - 100.00**
- ❏ RCA Victor 447-0601, picture sleeve, 1964......**100.00 - 200.00**
- ❏ RCA Victor 447-0601, black label, dog on left, 1965 **5.00 - 10.00**
- ❏ RCA Victor 447-0601, red label; Elvis' last name is spelled "Presely" on B-side, 1970 ....**4.00 - 8.00**
- ❏ RCA 447-0601, black label, dog near top, no "Victor" on label, 1977.....................**2.00 - 4.00**
- ❏ RCA PB-13891, from box "Elvis' Greatest Hits, Golden Singles, Volume 2"; gold vinyl, 1984..................**2.00 - 4.00**
- ❏ RCA PB-13891, picture sleeve, 1984.................**2.00 - 4.00**
- ❏ Collectables 80026, gray marbled vinyl, 1997..........**2.00 - 4.00**
- ❏ Sun 209, red vinyl, "DRE1-3051" in trail-off wax, from box "Elvis #1 Hit Singles Collection," 2001 ....**2.00 - 4.00**
- ❏ Sun 209, picture sleeve, "Sun ® Records is a registered trademark" on rear along lower left edge, 2001 .....**2.00 - 4.00**

There Goes My Everything/You'll Never Walk Alone

❑ RCA JB-13058, light yellow label promo, "Not for Sale"
on label, 1982 .... **7.50 - 15.00**

❑ RCA PB-13058, black label, dog near top, 1982 .... **2.50 - 5.00**

❑ RCA PB-13058, picture sleeve, 1982 .... **5.00 - 10.00**

There's a Honky Tonk Angel (Who Will Take Me Back In)/I Got a Feelin' in My Body

❏ RCA JB-11679, light yellow label promo, "Not for Sale" on label, 1979 .... **6.00 - 12.00**

❏ RCA PB-11679, black label, dog near top; has full production credits (background vocals, strings) listed in error on both sides, 1979 .... **7.50 - 15.00**

❑ RCA PB-11679, black label, dog near top; has production credits removed; only producers are listed, 1979 ....**2.50 - 5.00**

❑ RCA PB-11679, picture sleeve, 1979.................**5.00 - 10.00**

There's Always Me/Judy

❑ RCA Victor 47-9287, black label, dog on left, 1967 .. **5.00 - 10.00**

❑ RCA Victor 47-9287, white label promo, "Not for Sale" on label, 1967 ....**20.00 - 40.00**

❑ RCA Victor 47-9287, picture sleeve, 1967 ....**12.50 - 25.00**

❑ RCA Victor 447-0661, red label, 1970.................**7.50 - 15.00**

❑ RCA 447-0661, black label, dog near top, no "Victor" on label, 1977 ....**2.00 - 4.00**

This Is His Life: Elvis Presley

❑ RCA Victor (no number), promo-only picture sleeve; formerly, this was believed to have come with "I Want You, I Need You, I Love You," but now, consensus opinion now places it with promo copies of "Mystery Train," 1955 ....**750.00 – 1,500**

Too Much/Playing for Keeps

❏ RCA Victor 47-6800, East Coast pressing with horizontal
line on label, dog on label as usual, 1957 ....**15.00 - 30.00**

❏ RCA Victor 47-6800, East Coast pressing with horizontal
line on label, but with no dog, 1957 .... **100.00 - 200.00**

❑ RCA Victor 47-6800, Midwest or West Coast pressing without horizontal line on label, 1957 ....**15.00 - 30.00**

❑ RCA Victor 47-6800, picture sleeve, 1957 ....**45.00 - 90.00**

❑ RCA Victor 447-0617, black label, dog on top, 1959 **7.50 - 15.00**

❑ RCA Victor 447-0617, black label, dog on left, 1965 **5.00 - 10.00**

❑ RCA Victor 447-0617, orange label, 1969 ....**12.50 - 25.00**

❑ RCA Victor 447-0617, red label, 1970...................**4.00 - 8.00**

❑ RCA 447-0617, black label, dog near top, no "Victor" on label, 1977..**2.00 - 4.00**

❑ Collectables COL-4507, black vinyl, 1986..............**1.00 - 3.00**

❑ Collectables COL-4507, gold vinyl, 1992 ....**2.00 - 4.00**

❑ RCA Victor 47-6800, black label, dog on top, red vinyl, "DRE1-3037" in trail-off wax, from box "Elvis #1 Hit Singles Collection," 2001.................................**2.00 - 4.00**

❑ RCA Victor 47-6800, picture sleeve, "This is a replica of the original packaging" on rear along bottom, 2001....**2.00 - 4.00**

Tryin' to Get to You/I Love You Because

"Picture sleeves" of RCA Victor 47-6639 are bootlegs.

❑ RCA Victor 47-6639, East Coast pressing with horizontal
   line on label, 1956.....................................**35.00 - 70.00**

❑ RCA Victor 47-6639, Midwest or West Coast pressing
   without horizontal line on label, 1956 ....**35.00 - 70.00**

❑ RCA Victor 447-0612, black label, dog on top, 1959 **7.50 - 15.00**

❑ Collectables COL-4505, black vinyl, 1986...............**1.00 - 3.00**

❑ Collectables COL-4505, gold vinyl, 1992 ....**2.00 - 4.00**

20 Golden Hits in Full Color Sleeves

❑ RCA PP-11340,iIncludes 10 records (11099, 11100,
   11102, 11104-11109, 11111) and outer box, 1977**40.00 - 80.00**

U.S. Male/Stay Away

❑ RCA Victor 47-9465, black label, dog on left, 1968.. **5.00 - 10.00**

❑ RCA Victor 47-9465, yellow label promo, "Not for Sale"
   on label, 1968......................................**10.00 - 40.00**

❑ RCA Victor 47-9465, picture sleeve, 1968 ....**12.50 - 25.00**

❑ RCA Victor 447-0664, red label, 1970....................**4.00 - 8.00**

❑ RCA 447-0664, black label, dog near top, no "Victor"
on label, 1977..**2.50 - 5.00**

U.S. Male/Until It's Time for You to Go

❑ Collectables COL-4517, black vinyl, 1986...............**1.00 - 3.00**

❑ Collectables COL-4517, gold vinyl, 1992 ....**2.00 - 4.00**

Unchained Melody/Are You Sincere

❑ RCA GB-11988, Gold Standard Series, black label,
1980..**2.00 - 4.00**

Unchained Melody/Softly, As I Leave You

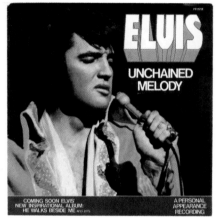

❏ RCA JH-11212, light yellow label promo, "Not for Sale"
   on label, 1978..**10.00 - 20.00**

❏ RCA PB-11212, black label, dog near top, erroneously states
   "Vocal Accompaniment by Sherrill Nielsen" on "Unchained
   Melody" side, 1978...**5.00 - 10.00**

❏ RCA PB-11212, black label, dog near top, no credit to
   Sherrill Nielsen on the "Unchained Melody" side,
   1978...**2.50 - 5.00**

❏ RCA PB-11212, picture sleeve, 1978......................**5.00 - 10.00**

**Until It's Time for You to Go/
We Can Make the Morning**

❏ RCA Victor 74-0619, orange label, 1971.................**3.00 - 6.00**

❏ RCA Victor 74-0619, yellow label promo, "Not for Sale"
on label, 1971 ....**15.00 - 30.00**

❏ RCA Victor 74-0619, picture sleeve, 1971 ....**7.50 - 15.00**

Viva Las Vegas/What'd I Say

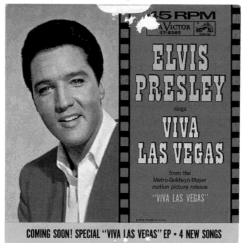

- ❏ RCA Victor 47-8360, black label, dog on top, 1964 .. **6.00 - 12.00**

- ❏ RCA Victor 47-8360, white label promo, "Not for Sale"
  on label, 1964 ....**25.00 - 50.00**

- ❏ RCA Victor 47-8360, picture sleeve, "Coming Soon!
  Special 'Viva Las Vegas' EP – 4 New Songs" on sleeve,
  1964 ....**12.50 - 25.00**

❑ RCA Victor 47-8360, picture sleeve, "Ask For Special
'Viva Las Vegas' EP – 4 New Songs" on sleeve,
1964...**25.00 - 50.00**

❑ RCA Victor 447-0646, black label, dog on top,
1965..**12.50 - 25.00**

❑ RCA Victor 447-0646, black label, dog on left,
1965..**5.00 - 10.00**

❑ RCA Victor 447-0646, orange label, 1969...........**12.50 - 25.00**

❑ RCA Victor 447-0646, red label, 1970.....................**4.00 - 8.00**

❑ RCA 447-0646, black label, dog near top, no "Victor"
on label, 1977...**2.00 - 4.00**

❑ RCA Victor 47-8360, black label, dog on top, red vinyl,
"DRE 13232" in trail-off wax, from box "Elvis Hit Singles
Collection, Volume 2," 2002..............................**2.00 - 4.00**

❑ RCA Victor 47-8360, picture sleeve, "Coming Soon! Special
'Viva Las Vegas' EP – 4 New Songs" on sleeve, "This is a
replica of the original packaging" on rear along lower
right edge, 2002...**2.00 - 4.00**

Way Down/My Way

❑ RCA GB-11504, black label, dog near top, 1979.......**2.00 - 4.00**

❑ Collectables 80023, gray marbled vinyl, 1997...........**2.00 - 4.00**

Way Down/Pledging My Love

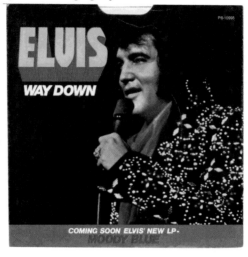

❏ RCA JB-10998, light yellow label promo, "Not for Sale"
on label, 1977..**10.00 - 20.00**

❏ RCA JB-10998, white label promo, "Elvis Presley" is twice
as large as the song titles, 1977.....................**60.00 - 120.00**

❏ RCA PB-10998, black label, dog near top, 1977........**2.50 - 5.00**

❏ RCA PB-10998, picture sleeve, 1977....................**5.00 - 10.00**

**Wear My Ring Around Your Neck/
Don'tcha Think It's Time**

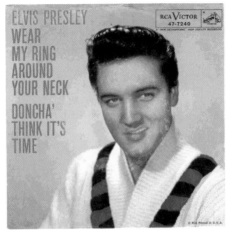

- ❑ RCA Victor 47-7240, black label, dog on top, 1958 **12.50 - 25.00**
- ❑ RCA Victor 47-7240, picture sleeve, 1958 ....**45.00 - 90.00**
- ❑ RCA Victor 447-0622, black label, dog on top, 1961 **6.00 - 12.00**
- ❑ RCA Victor 447-0622, black label, dog on left, 1965 **5.00 - 10.00**
- ❑ RCA Victor 447-0622, orange label, 1969 ....**12.50 - 25.00**
- ❑ RCA Victor 447-0622, red label, 1970.................**4.00 - 8.00**

❑ RCA 447-0622, black label, dog near top, no "Victor"
   on label, 1977...**2.00 - 4.00**

❑ Collectables 80027, gray marbled vinyl, 1997..........**2.00 - 4.00**

Where Did They Go, Lord/Rags to Riches

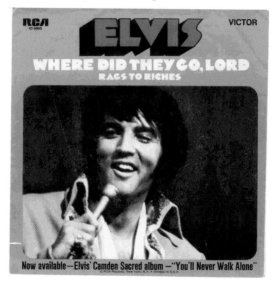

- ❑ RCA Victor 47-9980, orange label, 1971............**3.00 - 6.00**

- ❑ RCA Victor 47-9980, yellow label promo, "Not for Sale" on label, 1971...**15.00 - 30.00**

- ❑ RCA Victor 47-9980, picture sleeve, 1971 ....**10.00 - 20.00**

- ❑ RCA Victor 447-0680, red label, 1972..................**4.00 - 8.00**

- ❑ RCA 447-0680, black label, dog near top, no "Victor" on label, 1977...**2.00 - 4.00**

Witchcraft/Spinout

- ❑ Collectables 04764, 1997..................................**1.00 - 3.00**

The Wonder of You/Mama Liked the Roses

❏ RCA Victor 47-9835, orange label, 1970..............**4.00 - 8.00**

❏ RCA Victor 47-9835, yellow label promo, "Not for Sale"
on label, 1970...**15.00 - 30.00**

❑ RCA Victor 47-9835, picture sleeve, 1970 .... **7.50 - 15.00**

❑ RCA Victor 447-0676, red label, 1971 .... **4.00 - 8.00**

❑ RCA 447-0676, black label, dog near top,
   no "Victor" on label, 1977 .... **2.00 - 4.00**

❑ Collectables 80020, gray marbled vinyl, 1997 .... **2.00 - 4.00**

❑ RCA Victor 47-9835, orange label, red vinyl, "DRE 13230"
   in trail-off wax, from box "Elvis Hit Singles Collection,
   Volume 2," 2002 .... **2.00 - 4.00**

❑ RCA Victor 47-9835, picture sleeve, "This is a replica
   of the original packaging" on rear along lower
   right edge, 2002 .... **2.00 - 4.00**

You Don't Have to Say You Love Me/Patch It Up

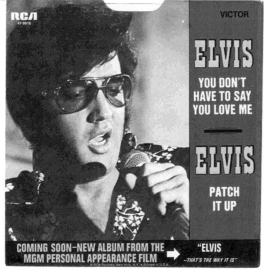

- ❑ RCA Victor 47-9916, orange label, 1970 ....**3.00 - 6.00**

- ❑ RCA Victor 47-9916, yellow label promo, "Not for Sale"
  on label, 1970 ....**12.50 - 25.00**

- ❑ RCA Victor 47-9916, picture sleeve, 1970 ....**7.50 - 15.00**

❑ RCA Victor 447-0678, red label, 1972..................**4.00 - 8.00**

❑ RCA 447-0678, black label, dog near top, no "Victor"
   on label, 1977...**2.00 - 4.00**

❑ Collectables 80024, gray marbled vinyl, 1997.........**2.00 - 4.00**

❑ RCA Victor 47-9916, orange label, red vinyl, "DRE 13227"
   in trail-off wax, from box "Elvis Hit Singles Collection,
   Volume 2," 2002 ....**2.00 - 4.00**

❑ RCA Victor 47-9916, picture sleeve, "This is a replica of the
   original packaging" on rear at bottom, 2002 ....**2.00 - 4.00**

You'll Never Walk Alone/We Call on Him

❑ RCA Victor 47-9600, black label, dog on left, 1968.. **6.00 - 12.00**

❑ RCA Victor 47-9600, yellow label promo,
   "Not for Sale" on label, 1968......................**15.00 - 30.00**

❑ RCA Victor 47-9600, picture sleeve, 1968 ....**50.00 - 100.00**

❑ RCA Victor 447-0665, red label, 1970.................**5.00 - 10.00**

❑ RCA 447-0665, black label, dog near top, no "Victor" on label,
   1977..**2.00 - 4.00**

You're a Heartbreaker/Milkcow Blues Boogie

See MILKCOW BLUES BOOGIE/YOU'RE A HEARTBREAKER.

**(You're the) Devil in Disguise/
Please Don't Drag That String Along**

❑ RCA Victor 47-8188, black label, dog on top, with incorrect B-side
title, 1963 .... **100.00 - 200.00**

**(You're the) Devil in Disguise/
Please Don't Drag That String Around**

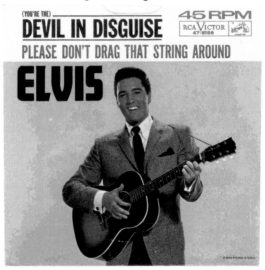

❏ RCA Victor 47-8188, black label, dog on top, with correct
    B-side title, 1963..**6.00 - 12.00**

❏ RCA Victor 47-8188, picture sleeve, all sleeves have correct
    B-side title, 1963..**15.00 - 30.00**

❏ RCA Victor 447-0641, black label, dog on top,
    1964...**12.50 - 25.00**

❏ RCA Victor 447-0641, black label, dog on left,
    1965..**5.00 - 10.00**

❏ RCA Victor 447-0641, red label, 1970...................**4.00 - 8.00**

❏ RCA 447-0641, black label, dog near top, no "Victor"
    on label, 1977...**2.00 - 4.00**

❏ RCA Victor 47-8188, black label, dog on top, red vinyl,
    "DRE 13235" in trail-off wax, from box "Elvis Hit Singles
    Collection, Volume 2," 2002 ....**2.00 - 4.00**

❏ RCA Victor 47-8188, picture sleeve, "This is a replica
    of the original packaging" on rear along lower
    right edge, 2002...**2.00 - 4.00**

78 RPM Singles

All Shook Up/That's When Your Heartaches Begin

❑ RCA Victor 20-6870, 1957.............................**50.00 - 100.00**

**Baby Let's Play House/
I'm Left, You're Right, She's Gone**

❑ Sun 217, 1955 ....**750.00 – 1,500.**

❑ RCA Victor 20-6383, 1955.............................**75.00 - 150.00**

Blue Moon/Just Because

❑ RCA Victor 20-6640, 1956.............................**50.00 - 100.00**

Blue Suede Shoes/Tutti Frutti

❑ RCA Victor 20-6636, 1956.............................**50.00 - 100.00**

Don't Be Cruel/Hound Dog

❑ RCA Victor 20-6604, 1956.............................**50.00 - 100.00**

Don't/I Beg of You

❑ RCA Victor 20-7150, 1958.............................**60.00 - 120.00**

Good Rockin' Tonight/I Don't Care If the Sun Don't Shine

❏ Sun 210, 1954 .... **900.00 – 1,800.**

❏ RCA Victor 20-6381, 1955 .... **75.00 - 150.00**

Hard Headed Woman/Don't Ask Me Why

❏ RCA Victor 20-7280, 1958..................**60.00 - 120.00**

Heartbreak Hotel/I Was the One

❏ RCA Victor 20-6420, 1956..................**50.00 - 100.00**

I Forgot to Remember to Forget/Mystery Train

❏ Sun 223, 1955 ....**500.00 – 1,000.**

❏ RCA Victor 20-6357, 1955..................**75.00 - 150.00**

I Got a Woman/I'm Countin' On You

❏ RCA Victor 20-6637, 1956..................**50.00 - 100.00**

I Want You, I Need You, I Love You/My Baby Left Me

❏ RCA Victor 20-6540, 1956..................**50.00 - 100.00**

I'm Gonna Sit Right Down and Cry (Over You)/I'll Never Let You Go (Little Darlin')

❏ RCA Victor 20-6638, 1956..................**50.00 - 100.00**

Jailhouse Rock/Treat Me Nice

❏ RCA Victor 20-7035, 1957.............................**50.00 - 100.00**

Lawdy Miss Clawdy/Shake, Rattle, and Roll

❏ RCA Victor 20-6642, 1956.............................**50.00 - 100.00**

(Let Me Be Your) Teddy Bear/Loving You

❏ RCA Victor 20-7000, 1957.............................**50.00 - 100.00**

Love Me Tender/Anyway You Want Me (That's How I Will Be)

❏ RCA Victor 20-6643, 1956.............................**50.00 - 100.00**

Milkcow Blues Boogie/You're a Heartbreaker

❏ Sun 215, 1955 ....**1,250 – 2,500**

❏ RCA Victor 20-6382, 1955.............................**75.00 - 150.00**

Money Honey/One-Sided Love Affair

❏ RCA Victor 20-6641, 1956.............................**50.00 - 100.00**

One Night/I Got Stung

❑ RCA Victor 20-7410, 1958.......................**250.00 - 500.00**

That's All Right/Blue Moon of Kentucky

❑ Sun 209, 1954 ....**1,500 – 3,000**

❑ RCA Victor 20-6380, 1955.......................**75.00 - 150.00**

Too Much/Playing for Keeps

❑ RCA Victor 20-6800, 1957.......................**50.00 - 100.00**

Tryin' to Get to You/I Love You Because

❑ RCA Victor 20-6639, 1956.......................**50.00 - 100.00**

Wear My Ring Around Your Neck/
Don'tcha Think It's Time

❑ RCA Victor 20-7240, 1958.......................**60.00 - 120.00**

7-Inch Extended Plays

Aloha from Hawaii Via Satellite

Contents: Something/You Gave Me a Mountain/I Can't Stop Loving You//My Way/What Now My Love/I'm So Lonesome I Could Cry

❑ RCA DTF0-2006, stereo jukebox issue; small hole, plays at 33 1/3 rpm, 1973.....................................**40.00 - 80.00**

❑ RCA DTF0-2006, picture sleeve, add 20 percent if an insert of 10 jukebox strips is there, 1973.........**50.00 - 100.00**

Anyway You Want Me

Contents: Anyway You Want Me (That's How I Will Be)/I'm Left, You're Right, She's Gone//I Don't Care if the Sun Don't Shine/ Mystery Train

❑ RCA Victor EPA-965, black label, dog on top, East Coast pressing with horizontal line on label, 1956 .....**20.00 - 40.00**

❑ RCA Victor EPA-965, black label, dog on top, East Coast pressing with horizontal line on label, but with no dog, 1956...**100.00 - 200.00**

❑ RCA Victor EPA-965, black label, dog on top, Midwest or West Coast pressing without horizontal line on label, 1956...**20.00 - 40.00**

❑ RCA Victor EPA-965, cardboard picture sleeve
with song titles and catalog number on front,
1956...**25.00 - 50.00**

❑ RCA Victor EPA-965, black label, dog on left, 1965.**15.00 - 30.00**

❑ RCA Victor EPA-965, cardboard picture sleeve without
song titles and catalog number on front, 1960s ..**20.00 - 40.00**

❑ RCA Victor EPA-965, orange label, 1969 ....**40.00 - 80.00**

Blue Moon of Kentucky/Love Me Tender// Mystery Train/ Milkcow Boogie Blues

❑ RCA Victor 599-9141, this is *"Side 6" and "Side 15"* of various
artists box set SPD-26, Great Country/Western Hits; notice the
erroneous title on the second side, 1957 ....**200.00 - 400.00**

Christmas with Elvis

Contents: White Christmas/Here Comes Santa Claus//Oh Little Town of
Bethlehem/Silent Night

❑ RCA Victor EPA-4340, black label, dog on top,
1958..**35.00 - 70.00**

❑ RCA Victor EPA-4340, cardboard picture sleeve, with
copyright notice and "Printed in U.S.A." at lower right,
1958..**40.00 - 80.00**

❑ RCA Victor EPA-4340, black label, dog on left,
1965..**20.00 - 40.00**

❑ RCA Victor EPA-4340, cardboard picture sleeve, without
copyright notice and "Printed in U.S.A." at lower right,
1965..**20.00 - 40.00**

❑ RCA Victor EPA-4340, orange label, 1969............**10.00 - 80.00**

Easy Come, Easy Go

Contents: Easy Come, Easy Go/The Love Machine/Yoga Is as Yoga Does//
You Gotta Shop/Sing You Children/I'll Take Love

❑ RCA Victor EPA-4387, black label, dog on left, 1967**15.00 - 30.00**

❑ RCA Victor EPA-4387, white label promo, 1967...**60.00 - 120.00**

❑ RCA Victor EPA-4387, picture sleeve, 1967............**15.00 - 30.00**

Elvis (Volume 1)

Contents: Rip It Up/Love Me//When My Blue Moon Turns to Gold Again/
Paralyzed

❑ RCA Victor EPA-992, black label, dog on top, East Coast
pressing with horizontal line on label, songwriting credit
on "Paralyzed" is "(Otis Blackwell)," 1956........**10.00 - 50.00**

❑ RCA Victor EPA-992, black label, dog on top, East Coast
   pressing with horizontal line on label; but with no dog,
   songwriting credit on "Paralyzed" is "(Otis Blackwell),"
   1956 .... **100.00 - 200.00**

❑ RCA Victor EPA-992, black label, dog on top,
   Midwest or West Coast pressing without horizontal line
   on label, songwriting credit on "Paralyzed" is "
   (Otis Blackwell-Elvis Presley)," 1956 .... **20.00 - 40.00**

❑ RCA Victor EPA-992, black label, dog on top,
   Midwest or West Coast pressing without horizontal line
   on label, songwriting credit on "Paralyzed" is
   "(Otis Blackwell)," 1956 .... **10.00 - 60.00**

❑ RCA Victor EPA-992, cardboard picture sleeve, titles
   at top of front cover, 1956 .... **25.00 - 50.00**

❑ RCA Victor EPA-992, black label, dog on left,
   1965 .... **15.00 - 30.00**

❑ RCA Victor EPA-992, cardboard picture sleeve,
   no titles at top of front cover, 1965 .... **30.00 - 60.00**

❑ RCA Victor EPA-992, orange label, 1969 .... **40.00 - 80.00**

Elvis (Volume 2)

Contents: So Glad You're Mine/Old Shep//Ready Teddy/Anyplace Is Paradise

❏ RCA Victor EPA-993, black label, dog on top,
    East Coast pressing with horizontal line on label,
    1956...**20.00 - 40.00**

❏ RCA Victor EPA-993, black label, dog on top,
    East Coast pressing with horizontal line on label,
    but with no dog, 1956 ....**100.00 - 200.00**

❏ RCA Victor EPA-993, black label, dog on top,
    Midwest or West Coast pressing without horizontal
    line on label, 1956...................................**20.00 - 40.00**

❏ RCA Victor EPA-993, cardboard picture sleeve,
    titles at top of front cover, 1956....................**25.00 - 50.00**

❏ RCA Victor EPA-993, black label, dog on left,
    1965...**15.00 - 30.00**

❏ RCA Victor EPA-993, cardboard picture sleeve, no titles
    at top of front cover, 1965...........................**15.00 - 30.00**

❏ RCA Victor EPA-993, orange label, 1969 ....**40.00 - 80.00**

Elvis By Request

Contents: Flaming Star/Summer Kisses, Winter Tears//Are You Lonesome To-Night?/It's Now or Never

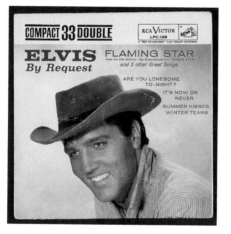

❑ RCA Victor LPC-128, "Compact 33 Double"
with small hole, 1961 ....**20.00 - 40.00**

❑ RCA Victor LPC-128, cardboard picture sleeve,
1961 ....**20.00 - 40.00**

Elvis Presley

RCA Victor EPA-747. Contents: Blue Suede Shoes/Tutti Frutti//I Got a Woman/Just Because

❑ RCA Victor EPA-747, black label, dog on top, East Coast pressing with horizontal line on label, 1956 ......**25.00 - 50.00**

❑ RCA Victor EPA-747, black label, dog on top, East Coast pressing with horizontal line on label, but with no dog, 1956 .... **100.00 - 200.00**

❑ RCA Victor EPA-747, black label, dog on top, Midwest or West Coast pressing without horizontal line on label; with incorrect label on Side 1 that lists, as song 3, "I'm Gonna Sit Right Down and Cry (Over You)," which does not appear on this record, 1956... **100.00 - 200.00**

❑ RCA Victor EPA-747, black label, dog on top, Midwest or West Coast pressing without horizontal line on label; with correct information on Side 1 label, 1956 ...**25.00 - 50.00**

❑ RCA Victor EPA-747, temporary envelope sleeve with dark blue print, "Blue Suede Shoes by Elvis Presley" in big letters; counterfeits have black print, 1956.................... **500.00 – 1,000.**

❑ RCA Victor EPA-747, cardboard picture sleeve, five different back covers exist, all with titles on front cover; any are of equal value, 1956...................................**25.00 - 50.00**

❑ RCA Victor EPA-747, black label, dog on left, 1965.**15.00 - 30.00**

❑ RCA Victor EPA-747, cardboard picture sleeve,
   no titles at top of front cover, 1965..................**15.00 - 30.00**

❑ RCA Victor EPA-747, orange label, 1969 ....**40.00 - 80.00**

Elvis Presley

RCA Victor EPA-830. Contents: Shake, Rattle and Roll/I Love You
Because//Blue Moon/ Lawdy, Miss Clawdy

❑ RCA Victor EPA-830, black label, dog on top, East Coast
   pressing with horizontal line on label, 1956 ......**25.00 - 50.00**

❑ RCA Victor EPA-830, black label, dog on top, East Coast
   pressing with horizontal line on label,
   but with no dog, 1956 ....**100.00 - 200.00**

❑ RCA Victor EPA-830, black label, dog on top,
   Midwest or West Coast pressing without horizontal
   line on label, 1956...................................**25.00 - 50.00**

❑ RCA Victor EPA-830, cardboard picture sleeve,
   titles at top of front cover, 1956.....................**25.00 - 50.00**

❑ RCA Victor EPA-830, black label, dog on left, 1965.**15.00 - 30.00**

❑ RCA Victor EPA-830, cardboard picture sleeve,
   no titles at top of front cover, 1965..................**15.00 - 30.00**

❑ RCA Victor EPA-830, orange label, 1969 ....**40.00 - 80.00**

Elvis Presley

RCA Victor EPB-1254. Contains two records with two songs on each side.

❏ RCA Victor 547-0793, Contents: Blue Suede Shoes/I'm Counting on You//I'm Gonna Sit Right Down and Cry (Over You)/I'll Never Let You Go; black label, dog on top, East Coast pressing with horizontal line on label, 1956 ....**50.00 - 100.00**

❏ RCA Victor 547-0793, same as above, except Midwest or West Coast pressing with no horizontal line on label, 1956..**50.00 - 100.00**

❏ RCA Victor 547-0794, Contents: Tutti Frutti/ Tryin' to Get to You//I Got a Woman/One Sided Love Affair; black label, dog on top, East Coast pressing with horizontal line on label, 1956 ....**50.00 - 100.00**

❏ RCA Victor 547-0794, same as above, except, Midwest or West Coast pressing with no horizontal line on label, 1956..**50.00 - 100.00**

❏ RCA Victor EPB-1254, cardboard double-pocket picture sleeve, with no mention of non-Elvis RCA Victor releases on back, 1956..**75.00 - 150.00**

❏ RCA Victor EPB-1254, cardboard double-pocket picture sleeve, any of three different back covers, each of equal value, with non-Elvis RCA Victor releases mentioned on back, 1956..**100.00 - 200.00**

Elvis Presley

RCA Victor SPD-22. Contains two records with two songs on each side. This was a giveaway to buyers of an "Elvis Presley" record player that cost $32.95 at retail.

❑ RCA Victor 599-9121, Contents: Blue Suede Shoes/I'm Counting on You//Tutti Frutti/Tryin' to Get to You; black label, dog on top; all known copies are East Coast pressings with horizontal line on label, 1956................................ **200.00 - 400.00**

❑ RCA Victor 599-9122, Contents: I Got a Woman/
One Sided Love Affair//I'm Gonna Sit Right Down and Cry
(Over You)/I'll Never Let You Go; black label, dog on top; all
known copies are East Coast pressings with horizontal line on
label, 1956 .... **200.00 - 400.00**

❑ RCA Victor SPD-22, double-pocket cardboard picture sleeve,
1956 .... **1,000 – 2,000**

Elvis Presley

RCA Victor SPD-23. Contains three records with two songs
on each side. This was a giveaway to buyers of an "Elvis Presley"
record player that cost $47.95 at retail.

❑ RCA Victor 599-9123, Contents: Blue Suede Shoes/I'm Counting
on You//Hound Dog/My Baby Left Me; black label, dog on top;
all known copies are East Coast pressings with horizontal line
on label, 1956 .... **300.00 - 600.00**

❑ RCA Victor 599-9124, Contents: I Got a Woman/One Sided Love
Affair//Don't Be Cruel/I Want You, I Need You, I Love You; black
label, dog on top; all known copies are East Coast pressings
with horizontal line on label, 1956 .... **300.00 - 600.00**

❑ RCA Victor 599-9125, Contents: I'm Gonna Sit Right Down and
Cry (Over You)/I'll Never Let You Go// Tutti Frutti/Tryin' to Get
to You; black label, dog on top; all known copies are East Coast
pressings with horizontal line on label, 1956 . **300.00 - 600.00**

❑ RCA Victor SPD-23, triple-pocket cardboard picture sleeve,
    1956 . . . .**1,000 – 3,000**

Elvis Presley... the most talked-about new personality in the last ten years of recorded music

RCA Victor EPB-1254. Contains two records with three songs on each
side. This was sent only to radio stations.

❑ RCA Victor 547-0793, Contents: Blue Suede Shoes/I'm Counting
    on You/I Got a Woman//I'll Never Let You Go (Little Darlin')/
    Blue Moon/Money Honey; black label, dog on top; all known
    copies are Midwest or West Coast pressings without horizontal
    line on label, 1956 . . . . **500.00 – 1,000**

❑ RCA Victor 547-0794, Contents: One Sided Love Affair/I Love
    You Because/Just Because//Tutti Frutti/Tryin' to Get to You/I'm
    Gonna Sit Right Down and Cry (Over You); black label, dog
    on top; all known copies are Midwest or West Coast pressings
    without horizontal line on label, 1956 . . . . **500.00 – 1,000**

❑ RCA Victor EPB-1254, picture sleeve, green print on white
    background; some counterfeits have black print, others have a
    gray background, 1956 . . . .**2,000 – 3,000**

Elvis Sails

Contents: Press Interview with Elvis Presley//Elvis Presley's Newsreel Interview/Pat Hernon Interviews Elvis in the Library of the U.S.S. Randall at Sailing

❏ RCA Victor EPA-4325, black label, dog on top; all authentic copies have machine-stamped trail-off numbers, 1958 .... **40.00 - 80.00**

❏ RCA Victor EPA-4325, cardboard picture sleeve, with 1959 calendar and a hole to make it suitable for hanging, 1958 .... **40.00 - 80.00**

❏ RCA Victor EPA-5157, black label, dog on top, 1965 .... **15.00 - 30.00**

❏ RCA Victor EPA-5157, cardboard picture sleeve, 1965 .... **15.00 - 30.00**

❏ RCA Victor EPA-5157, orange label, 1969 .... **40.00 - 80.00**

Elvis Sings Christmas Songs

Contents: Santa Bring My Baby Back (To Me)/Blue Christmas//Santa Claus Is Back in Town/I'll Be Home for Christmas

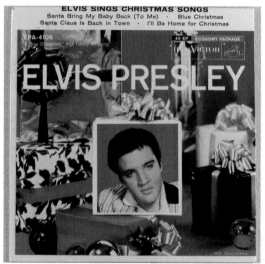

❑ RCA Victor EPA-4108, black label, dog on top, 1957 **20.00 - 40.00**

❑ RCA Victor EPA-4108, cardboard picture sleeve, similar for all editions, 1957 .... **20.00 - 40.00**

❏ RCA Victor EPA-4108, black label, dog on left, 1965...**15.00 - 30.00**

❏ RCA Victor EPA-4108, orange label, 1969............**40.00 - 80.00**

Follow That Dream

Contents: Follow That Dream/Angel//What a Wonderful Life/I'm Not the Marrying Kind

❏ RCA Victor EPA-4368, black label, dog on top,
    no times on label, 1962...........................**15.00 - 30.00**

❏ RCA Victor EPA-4368, black label, dog on top,
    with times on label, 1962 ....**20.00 - 40.00**

❏ RCA Victor EPA-4368, cardboard picture sleeve; "Follow That
    Dream" is listed as 1:35, "Angel" is listed as 2:35, and "I'm Not
    the Marrying Kind" is listed as 1:49, 1962 ....**20.00 - 40.00**

❏ RCA Victor EPA-4368, paper sleeve with "Coin Operator --
    DJ Prevue" at top; print is in red; counterfeits have
    black print, 1962....................................**75.00 - 150.00**

❏ RCA Victor EPA-4368, black label, dog on left, 1965...**12.50 - 25.00**

❏ RCA Victor EPA-4368, cardbvoard picture sleeve,
    "Follow That Dream" is listed as 1:38, "Angel"
    is listed as 2:40, and "I'm Not the Marrying Kind"
    is listed as 2:00, 1965 ....**12.50 - 25.00**

❏ RCA Victor EPA-4368, orange label, 1969............**40.00 - 80.00**

Heartbreak Hotel

Contents: Heartbreak Hotel/I Was the One//Money Honey/I Forgot to Remember to Forget

❑ RCA Victor EPA-821, black label, dog on top,
   East Coast pressing with horizontal line on label,
   1956...**25.00 - 50.00**

❑ RCA Victor EPA-821, black label, dog on top,
   East Coast pressing with horizontal line on label,
   but with no dog, 1956 ....**100.00 - 200.00**

❑ RCA Victor EPA-821, black label, dog on top,
   Midwest or West Coast pressing without horizontal
   line on label, 1956...............................**25.00 - 50.00**

❑ RCA Victor EPA-821, cardboard picture sleeve,
   similar for all editions, 1956 ....**25.00 - 50.00**

❑ RCA Victor EPA-821, black label, dog on left,
   1965..**15.00 - 30.00**

❑ RCA Victor EPA-821, orange label, 1969 ....**40.00 - 80.00**

HEARTBREAK HOTEL

Contents: Heartbreak Hotel/I Was the One//Heartbreak Hotel
(Alternate Take 5)/I Was the One (Alternate Take 2)

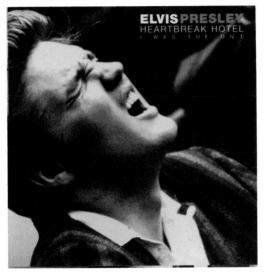

❑ RCA 07863-64476-7, 1996 ....**1.00 - 3.00**

❑ RCA 07863-64476-7, glossy paper picture sleeve,
   1996...**1.00 - 3.00**

Jailhouse Rock

Contents: Jailhouse Rock/Young and Beautiful//I Want to Be Free/
Don't Leave Me Now/(You're So Square) Baby I Don't Care

❑ RCA Victor EPA-4114, black label, dog on top,
    1957...**20.00 - 40.00**

❑ RCA Victor EPA-4114, cardboard picture sleeve,
    1957...**20.00 - 40.00**

❑ RCA Victor EPA-4114, black label, dog on left,
    1965...**15.00 - 30.00**

❑ RCA Victor EPA-4114, orange label, 1969............**40.00 - 80.00**

Just for You (Elvis Presley)

Contents: I Need You So/Have I Told You Lately//Blueberry Hill/Is It So
Strange

❑ RCA Victor EPA-4041, black label, dog on top, East Coast
    pressing with horizontal line on label, 1957 ......**25.00 - 50.00**

❑ RCA Victor EPA-4041, black label, dog on top,
    East Coast pressing with horizontal line on label,
    but with no dog, 1957 ....**100.00 - 200.00**

❑ RCA Victor EPA-4041, black label, dog on top, Midwest or
West Coast pressing without horizontal line on label,
1957...**25.00 - 50.00**

❑ RCA Victor EPA-4041, cardboard picture sleeve, similar
for all editions, 1957.............................**25.00 - 50.00**

❑ RCA Victor EPA-4041, black label, dog on left,
1965...**15.00 - 30.00**

❑ RCA Victor EPA-4041, orange label, 1969...........**40.00 - 80.00**

Kid Galahad

Contents: King of the Whole Wide World/This Is Living/Riding the
Rainbow//Home Is Where the Heart Is/I Got Lucky/A Whistling Tune

❑ RCA Victor EPA-4371, black label, dog on top,
1962...**20.00 - 40.00**

❑ RCA Victor EPA-4371, cardboard picture sleeve,
similar for all editions, 1962.......................**20.00 - 40.00**

❑ RCA Victor EPA-4371, black label, dog on left,
1965...**15.00 - 30.00**

❑ RCA Victor EPA-4371, orange label, 1969...........**40.00 - 80.00**

King Creole

Contents: King Creole/New Orleans//As Long as I Have You/Lover Doll

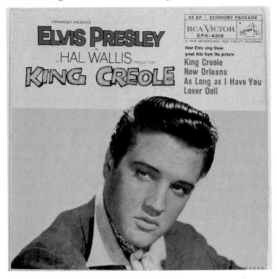

❑ RCA Victor EPA-4319, black label, dog on top,
  1958..**20.00 - 40.00**

❑ RCA Victor EPA-4319, cardboard picture sleeve,
  without copyright notice on front cover, 1958.....**20.00 - 40.00**

- ❏ RCA Victor EPA-4319, cardboard picture sleeve, with copyright notice on front cover, 1958.........**25.00 - 50.00**

- ❏ RCA Victor EPA-5122, maroon label, 1959..........**1,500 – 2,000**

- ❏ RCA Victor EPA-5122, black label, dog on top, 1959**15.00 - 30.00**

- ❏ RCA Victor EPA-5122, cardboard picture sleeve, with "Gold Standard Series" on front cover, 1959......**20.00 - 40.00**

- ❏ RCA Victor EPA-5122, black label, dog on left, 1965**12.50 - 25.00**

- ❏ RCA Victor EPA-5122, cardboard picture sleeve, without "Gold Standard Series" on front cover, 1965......**15.00 - 30.00**

- ❏ RCA Victor EPA-5122, orange label, 1969...........**40.00 - 80.00**

King Creole, Vol. 2

Contents: Trouble/Young Dreams//Crawfish/Dixieland Rock

- ❏ RCA Victor EPA-4321, black label, dog on top, 1958...**20.00 - 40.00**

- ❏ RCA Victor EPA-4321, cardboard picture sleeve, similar for all editions, 1958.......................**20.00 - 40.00**

- ❏ RCA Victor EPA-4321, black label, dog on left, 1965...**15.00 - 30.00**

- ❏ RCA Victor EPA-4321, orange label, 1969...........**40.00 - 80.00**

Love Me Tender

Contents: Love Me Tender/Let Me//Poor Boy/We're Gonna Move

❑ RCA Victor EPA-4006, black label, dog on top, East Coast
   pressing with horizontal line on label, 1956 ......**25.00 - 50.00**

❑ RCA Victor EPA-4006, black label, dog on top, East Coast
   pressing with horizontal line on label, but with no dog,
   1956...**100.00 - 200.00**

❑ RCA Victor EPA-4006, black label, dog on top,
   Midwest or West Coast pressing without horizontal
   line on label, 1956...................................**25.00 - 50.00**

❑ RCA Victor EPA-4006, cardboard picture sleeve,
   with song titles on top of front cover, 1956 ....**25.00 - 50.00**

❑ RCA Victor EPA-4006, black label, dog on left,
   1965..**15.00 - 30.00**

❑ RCA Victor EPA-4006, cardboard picture sleeve,
   no song titles on top of front cover, 1965 ....**15.00 - 30.00**

❑ RCA Victor EPA-4006, orange label, 1969............**40.00 - 80.00**

Love Me Tender/Anyway You Want Me (That's How I Will Be)//Welcome to the Club/ I Won't Be Rockin' Tonight

❏ RCA Victor DJ-7, white label promo; B-side
   by Jean Chapel; the Elvis Presley side also has the number
   "47-6643"; the Jean Chapel side also has the number
   "47-6681," 1956 ....**100.00 - 200.00**

Loving You, Vol. I

Contents: Loving You/Party//(Let Me Be Your) Teddy Bear/True Love

❏ RCA Victor EPA-1-1515, black label, dog on top, East Coast
   pressing with horizontal line on label, 1957 ......**20.00 - 40.00**

❏ RCA Victor EPA-1-1515, black label, dog on top,
   Midwest or West Coast pressing without horizontal
   line on label, 1957....................................**20.00 - 40.00**

❏ RCA Victor EPA-1-1515, cardboard picture sleeve,
   similar for all editions, 1957 ....**20.00 - 40.00**

❏ RCA Victor EPA-1-1515, black label, dog on left,
   1965..**15.00 - 30.00**

❏ RCA Victor EPA-1-1515, orange label, 1969 ....**40.00 - 80.00**

Loving You, Vol. II

Contents: Lonesome Cowboy/Hot Dog//Mean Woman Blues/Got a Lot of Livin' to Do

❑ RCA Victor EPA-2-1515, black label, dog on top, East Coast pressing with horizontal line on label, 1957 ......**20.00 - 40.00**

❑ RCA Victor EPA-2-1515, black label, dog on top, Midwest or West Coast pressing without horizontal line on label, 1957 ....**20.00 - 40.00**

❑ RCA Victor EPA-2-1515, cardboard picture sleeve, with song titles on top of front cover, 1957 ....**20.00 - 40.00**

❑ RCA Victor EPA-2-1515, black label, dog on left, 1965 ....**15.00 - 30.00**

❑ RCA Victor EPA-2-1515, cardboard picture sleeve, no song titles on top of front cover, 1965 ....**15.00 - 30.00**

❑ RCA Victor EPA-2-1515, orange label, 1969 ....**40.00 - 80.00**

Peace in the Valley

Contents: (There'll Be) Peace in the Valley (For Me)/It Is No Secret (What God Can Do)//I Believe/Take My Hand, Precious Lord

❏ RCA Victor EPA-4054, black label, dog on top, East Coast pressing with horizontal line on label, 1957 ......**20.00 - 40.00**

❏ RCA Victor EPA-4054, black label, dog on top,
   Midwest or West Coast pressing without horizontal line
   on label, 1957...**20.00 - 40.00**

❏ RCA Victor EPA-4054, cardboard picture sleeve,
   1957...**20.00 - 40.00**

❏ RCA Victor EPA-5121, maroon label, 1959.......**200.00 - 400.00**

❏ RCA Victor EPA-5121, black label, dog on top,
   1959...**15.00 - 30.00**

❏ RCA Victor EPA-5121, cardboard picture sleeve,
   three slightly different cover variations with no difference
   in value, 1959...**20.00 - 40.00**

❏ RCA Victor EPA-5121, black label, dog on left,
   1965...**12.50 - 25.00**

❏ RCA Victor EPA-5121, orange label, 1969...........**40.00 - 80.00**

Perfect for Parties

Elvis Presley introduces three songs on each side, only one on each of which is an Elvis song; because of his pervasive appearance on this record, it is listed.

❑ RCA Victor SPA-7-37, black label, dog on top, East Coast pressing with horizontal line on label; white label copies are counterfeits, 1956...................................**30.00 - 60.00**

❑ RCA Victor SPA-7-37, black label, dog on top, Midwest or West Coast pressing without horizontal line on label; white label copies are counterfeits, 1956 ....**30.00 - 60.00**

❑ RCA Victor SPA-7-37, thin cardboard picture sleeve; counterfeits are made of thick cardboard, 1956 ....**30.00 - 60.00**

The Real Elvis

Contents: Don't Be Cruel/I Want You, I Need You, I Love You//Hound Dog/My Baby Left Me

❑ RCA Victor EPA-940, East Coast pressing with horizontal line on label, 1956 ....**25.00 - 50.00**

❑ RCA Victor EPA-940, East Coast pressing with horizontal line on label, but with no dog, 1956 .... **100.00 - 200.00**

❑ RCA Victor EPA-940, Midwest or West Coast pressing without horizontal line on label, 1956 ....**25.00 - 50.00**

❑ RCA Victor EPA-940, cardboard picture sleeve, 1956 ....**25.00 - 50.00**

❑ RCA Victor EPA-5120, maroon label, 1959 ...... **300.00 - 600.00**

❑ RCA Victor EPA-5120, black label, dog on top, 1959 ....**30.00 - 60.00**

❑ RCA Victor EPA-5120, cardboard picture sleeve, similar for all editions, 1959 ....**30.00 - 60.00**

❑ RCA Victor EPA-5120, black label, dog on left,
  1965...**12.50 - 25.00**

❑ RCA Victor EPA-5120, orange label, 1969...........**40.00 - 80.00**

Strictly Elvis (Elvis, Vol. 3)

Contents: Long Tall Sally/First in Line//How Do You Think I Feel/
How's the World Treating You

❑ RCA Victor EPA-994, East Coast pressing with horizontal
  line on label, 1956.....................................**25.00 - 50.00**

❑ RCA Victor EPA-994, East Coast pressing with horizontal
  line on label, but with no dog, 1956............**100.00 - 200.00**

❑ RCA Victor EPA-994, Midwest or West Coast pressing
  without horizontal line on label, 1956............**25.00 - 50.00**

❑ RCA Victor EPA-994, cardboard picture sleeve,
  with titles listed on front cover, 1956...............**25.00 - 50.00**

❑ RCA Victor EPA-994, black label, dog on left, 1965.**15.00 - 30.00**

❑ RCA Victor EPA-994, cardboard picture sleeve,
  no titles listed on front cover, 1965...................**15.00 - 30.00**

❑ RCA Victor EPA-994, orange label, 1969 ....**40.00 - 80.00**

Tickle Me

Contents: I Feel That I've Known You Forever/
Slowly but Surely//Night Rider/Dirty Feeling

❑ RCA Victor EPA-4383, black label, dog on left, 1965.**15.00 - 30.00**

❏ RCA Victor EPA-4383, cardboard picture sleeve,
  "Coming Soon! Special Elvis Anniversary Album"
  on front cover, 1965....................................**15.00 - 30.00**

❏ RCA Victor EPA-4383, cardboard picture sleeve,
  "Ask for Special Elvis Anniversary Album"
  on front cover, 1965....................................**15.00 - 30.00**

❏ RCA Victor EPA-4383, orange label, 1969............**40.00 - 80.00**

❏ RCA Victor EPA-4383, cardboard picture sleeve,
  no blurb for new album on front cover, 1969.....**20.00 - 40.00**

Too Much/Playing for Keeps//Chantez-Chantez/ Honkytonk Heart

❏ RCA Victor DJ-56, white label promo, B-side by Dinah Shore;
  the Elvis Presley side also has the number "47-6800";
  the Dinah Shore side also has the number "47-6792,"
  1957 .... **100.00 - 200.00**

A Touch of Gold

Contents: Hard Headed Woman/Good Rockin' Tonight//Don't/
I Beg of You

❏ RCA Victor EPA-5088, maroon label, 1959....... **200.00 - 400.00**

❏ RCA Victor EPA-5088, black label, dog on top,
  1959..**30.00 - 60.00**

❏ RCA Victor EPA-5088, cardboard picture sleeve,
    similar for all editions, 1959 ....**30.00 - 60.00**

❏ RCA Victor EPA-5088, black label, dog on left, 1965**15.00 - 30.00**

❏ RCA Victor EPA-5088, orange label, 1969............**40.00 - 80.00**

A Touch of Gold, Volume II

Contents: Wear My Ring Around Your Neck/Treat Me Nice//One Night/
That's All Right

❏ RCA Victor EPA-5101, maroon label, 1959.......**200.00 - 400.00**

❏ RCA Victor EPA-5101, black label, dog on top,
    1959...**30.00 - 60.00**

❏ RCA Victor EPA-5101, cardboard picture sleeve,
    similar for all editions, 1959 ....**30.00 - 60.00**

❏ RCA Victor EPA-5101, black label, dog on left,
    1965...**15.00 - 30.00**

❏ RCA Victor EPA-5101, orange label, 1969............**40.00 - 80.00**

A Touch of Gold, Volume 3

Contents: All Shook Up/Don't Ask Me Why//Too Much/Blue Moon of
Kentucky

❏ RCA Victor EPA-5141, maroon label, 1959.......**200.00 - 400.00**

❏ RCA Victor EPA-5141, black label, dog on top, 1959
    ....**35.00 - 70.00**

❏ RCA Victor EPA-5141, cardboard picture sleeve, similar for all
   editions, 1959 ....**35.00 - 70.00**

❏ RCA Victor EPA-5141, black label, dog on left, 1965 **15.00 - 30.00**

❏ RCA Victor EPA-5141, orange label, 1969 ....**40.00 - 80.00**

TV Guide Presents Elvis Presley

❏ RCA Victor G8-MW-8705, promo only, light blue label, locked
   grooves (tone arm has to be moved manually to play each of
   the four excerpts); counterfeits are continuous play (record
   plays through to the end without having to manually move the
   tone arm), 1956 ....**600.00 – 1,200**

Viva Las Vegas

Contents: If You Think I Don't Need You/I Need Somebody to Lean On/
/C'mon Everybody/Today, Tomorrow and Forever

❏ RCA Victor EPA-4382, black label, dog on top,
   1964 ....**20.00 - 40.00**

❏ RCA Victor EPA-4382, cardboard picture sleeve,
   similar for all editions, 1964 ....**20.00 - 40.00**

❏ RCA Victor EPA-4382, black label, dog on left,
   1965 ....**15.00 - 30.00**

❏ RCA Victor EPA-4382, orange label, 1969 ....**40.00 - 80.00**

12-Inch Singles

A Little Less Conversation

Contents: 12" Extended Remix//Radio Remix Edit/Original Version

❑ RCA 07863-60570-1, credited to "Elvis vs JXL," price includes
record and custom cover, 2002......................**6.00 - 12.00**

Little Sister/Rip It Up

❑ RCA EP-0517, white label promo, 1983 ....**50.00 - 100.00**

RUBBERNECKIN'

Contents: Paul Oakenfold Remix 12" Extended//Paul Oakenfold Remix
Radio Edit/Original Version

❑ RCA 82876-54218-1, stock copy, price includes
record and custom cover, 2003......................**6.00 - 12.00**

❑ RCA HEAB-54262-1, promo, black label,
comes in generic black sleeve with custom
sticker at upper right, 2003..........................**25.00 - 50.00**

Albums

Almost in Love

❑ RCA Camden CAS-2440, last song on Side 2 is
"Stay Away, Joe", 1970.....................................**20.00 - 40.00**

❑ RCA Camden CAS-2440, last song on Side 2 is
"Stay Away", 1973...**12.50 - 25.00**

❑ Pickwick CAS-2440, 1975 ....**5.00 - 10.00**

Aloha from Hawaii Via Satellite

❑ RCA Victor VPSX-6089, two-record set, quadraphonic,
dark orange labels with "QuadraDisc" on top and
"RCA" on bottom; the Saturn-shaped logo on the
back cover does not list the songs on the album,
1973...**50.00 - 100.00**

❑ RCA Victor VPSX-6089, two-record set, quadraphonic,
promo only; dark orange labels with "QuadraDisc"
on top and ""RCA" on bottom; the Saturn-shaped
logo on the back cover does not list the songs on the
album, two white stickers on front cover list the
contents and times, 1973...........................**1,000 – 2,000**

❑ RCA Victor VPSX-6089, two-record set, quadraphonic, dark orange labels with "QuadraDisc" on top and ""RCA" on bottom; the Saturn-shaped logo on the back cover does not list the songs on the album, with Saturn-shaped sticker on front or back cover that DOES list the contents and "QuadraDisc" black and gold sticker at upper left front, 1973 ....**50.00 - 100.00**

❑ RCA Victor VPSX-6089, two-record set, quadraphonic; promo only; Stokely-Van Camp employee version with Saturn-shaped sticker added to front shrink wrap with "Chicken of the Sea" and mermaid logo; counterfeits exist of the sticker; be suspicious if the sticker is actually attached to the cover, as it was only attached to the shrink wrap, 1973 ......**3,500 – 5,000**

❑ RCA Victor VPSX-6089, two-record set, quadraphonic; dark orange labels with "QuadraDisc" on top and ""RCA" on bottom; cover now says "QuadraDisc" at lower right front, and the Saturn-shaped logo on the back now has the complete contents within it, 1973..**25.00 - 50.00**

❑ RCA Victor R 213736, two-record set, stereo; RCA Record Club edition; orange labels, 1973 ....**35.00 - 70.00**

❑ RCA Victor VPSX-6089, two-record set, quadraphonic; lighter orange labels with "RCA" at side and "QuadraDisc" at bottom; cover now says "QuadraDisc" at lower right front, and the Saturn-shaped logo on the back now has the complete contents within it, 1974..**20.00 - 40.00**

❑ RCA Victor CPD2-2642, two-record set, quadraphonic;
   lighter orange labels with "RCA" at side and "QuadraDisc"
   at bottom; new catalog number, 1975 ....**15.00 - 30.00**

❑ RCA Victor R 213736, two-record set, stereo;
   RCA Record Club edition; tan labels, 1975 ....**30.00 - 60.00**

❑ RCA Victor CPD2-2642, two-record set, quadraphonic;
   black labels, dog near top, 1977 ....**40.00 - 80.00**

❑ RCA Victor R 213736, two-record set, stereo;
   RCA Record Club edition; black labels,
   dog near top, 1977 ....**15.00 - 30.00**

❑ RCA Victor CPL2-2642, two-record set, stereo; black labels,
   dog near top, "Victor" at left; single-pocket jacket,
   1984..**6.00 - 12.00**

❑ RCA Victor CPL2-2642, two-record set, stereo, red vinyl,
   "DRL" number in trail-off wax, "BMG Special Products"
   logo on back cover, from box "Elvis Top Album Collection
   Volume 2," 2003 ....**10.00 - 20.00**

The Alternate Aloha

❑ RCA 6985-1-R, 1988 ....**10.00 - 20.00**

Always on My Mind

❑ RCA Victor AFL1-5430, purple vinyl, 1985 ....**10.00 - 20.00**

❑ RCA Victor AFL1-5430, black vinyl, 1985 ....**7.50 - 15.00**

Back in Memphis

❑ RCA Victor LSP-4429, orange label, non-flexible vinyl,
1970..**20.00 - 40.00**

❑ RCA Victor LSP-4429, orange label, flexible vinyl,
1971...**15.00 - 30.00**

❑ RCA Victor LSP-4429, tan label, 1975.................**12.50 - 25.00**

❑ RCA Victor LSP-4429, black label, dog near top, 1977.........**7.50
- 15.00**

❑ RCA Victor AFL1-4429, black label, dog near top,
"Victor" at left; with sticker wrapped around spine
with new number, 1977 ....**6.00 - 12.00**

❑ RCA Victor AYL1-3892, black label, dog near top, "Victor"
at left, 1980...**5.00 - 10.00**

Beginning (1954-1955)

❏ Marvenco 101, pink vinyl with booklet and facsimile contract, 1988...**10.00 - 20.00**

❏ Marvenco 101, black vinyl with booklet and facsimile contract, 1988...**7.50 - 15.00**

Beginning Years

❏ Louisiana Hayride LH-3061, with booklet and facsimile contract, 1984...**10.00 - 20.00**

Blue Hawaii

❏ RCA Victor LPM-2426, mono, "Long Play" on label; with sticker on cover advertising the presence of "Can't Help Falling in Love" and "Rock-a-Hula Baby," 1961.............**50.00 - 100.00**

❏ RCA Victor LSP-2426, stereo, "Living Stereo" on label and upper right front cover; with sticker on cover advertising the presence of "Can't Help Falling in Love" and "Rock-a-Hula Baby," 1961......................**75.00 - 150.00**

❏ RCA Victor LPM-2426, mono, "Long Play" on label; no sticker on front cover, 1962...**30.00 - 60.00**

❏ RCA Victor LSP-2426, stereo, "Living Stereo" on label and upper right front cover; no sticker on front cover, 1962.**40.00 - 80.00**

❏ RCA Victor LPM-2426, mono, "Mono" on label,
1963...**25.00 - 50.00**

❏ RCA Victor LSP-2426, stereo, "Stereo" on label;
"Victor Stereo" on upper right front cover, 1964..**25.00 - 50.00**

❏ RCA Victor LPM-2426, mono, "Monaural" on label,
1964...**20.00 - 40.00**

❏ RCA Victor LSP-2426, stereo, orange label, non-flexible vinyl,
1968...**20.00 - 40.00**

❏ RCA Victor LSP-2426, stereo, orange label, flexible vinyl,
1971...**50.00 - 20.00**

❏ RCA Victor LSP-2426, stereo, tan label, 1975........**50.00 - 20.00**

❏ RCA Victor LSP-2426, stereo, black label, dog near top,
"Victor" at left, 1977 ....**6.00 - 12.00**

❏ RCA Victor LSP-2426, stereo, blue vinyl, experimental
pressing; black label, dog near top, "Victor"
at left, 1977...**500.00 – 1,000.**

❏ RCA Victor AFL1-2426, stereo, black label, dog near top;
some copies have sticker wrapped around spine with
new number, 1977......................................**6.00 - 12.00**

❑ RCA Victor AYL1-3683, stereo, black label, dog near top,
"Victor" at left; some copies have sticker wrapped
around spine with new number, 1980 .... **5.00 - 10.00**

❑ RCA Victor LSP-2426, stereo, red vinyl, "DRL 13358"
in trail-off wax, "BMG Special Products" logo on
back cover, from box "Elvis Top Album Collection
Volume 1," 2003 .... **10.00 - 20.00**

Burning Love And Hits from His Movies, Vol. 2

❑ RCA Camden CAS-2595, with front cover advertisement
for bonus photo, 1972 .... **12.50 - 25.00**

❑ RCA Camden CAS-2595, bonus photo, 1972,
add this to above .... **12.50 - 25.00**

❑ RCA Camden CAS-2595, no advertisement on cover,
no bonus photo, 1972 .... **5.00 - 10.00**

❑ Pickwick CAS-2595, with notice about the upcoming
"Aloha from Hawaii" show on back cover, which
had long since happened by then, 1975 .... **6.00 - 12.00**

❑ Pickwick CAS-2595, without "Aloha from Hawaii"
notice on back, 1976 .... **4.00 - 8.00**

C'mon Everybody

❑ RCA Camden CAL-2518, 1971 ....**10.00 - 20.00**

❑ Pickwick CAS-2518, 1975 ....**5.00 - 10.00**

A Canadian Tribute

❑ RCA Victor KKL1-7065, gold vinyl, embossed cover,
1978...**10.00 - 20.00**

Clambake

❑ RCA Victor LPM-3893, mono, 1967 ....**125.00 - 250.00**

❑ RCA Victor LSP-3893, stereo, 1967 ....**30.00 - 60.00**

❑ RCA Victor LPM/LSP-3893, bonus photo with
either of above, 1967.......................................**25.00 - 50.00**

❑ RCA Victor APL1-2565, black label, dog near top,
1977...**6.00 - 12.00**

Collectors Gold

❑ RCA 3114-1-R, three-record boxed set, 1991 ....**100.00 - 200.00**

The Complete Sun Sessions

❑ RCA 6414-1-R, two-record set, 1987 ....**15.00 - 30.00**

Country Classics

❏ RCA Victor R 233299(e), two-record set, only offered through
RCA Music Service, 1980 ....**20.00 - 40.00**

Country Memories

❏ RCA Victor R 244069, two-record set, only offered through RCA
Music Service, 1978 ....**20.00 - 40.00**

Country Music

❏ Time-Life STW-106, 1981 ....**10.00 - 20.00**

A Date with Elvis

❏ RCA Victor LPM-2011, mono, "Long Play" on label;
gatefold cover, no sticker on front cover, 1959 **200.00 - 400.00**

❏ RCA Victor LPM-2011, mono, "Long Play" on label; gatefold
cover, with sticker on front cover, 1959.........**250.00 - 500.00**

❏ RCA Victor LPM-2011, mono, "Mono" on label; standard cover,
1963..**50.00 - 100.00**

❏ RCA Victor LPM-2011, mono, "Monaural" on label,
1965..**25.00 - 50.00**

❑ RCA Victor LSP-2011(e), stereo, black label,
   "RCA Victor" above dog; "Stereo Electronically
   Reprocessed" on label, 1965 ....**25.00 - 50.00**

❑ RCA Victor LSP-2011(e), stereo, orange label,
   non-flexible vinyl, 1968 ....**15.00 - 30.00**

❑ RCA Victor LSP-2011(e), stereo, orange label,
   flexible vinyl, 1971 ....**10.00 - 20.00**

❑ RCA Victor LSP-2011(e), stereo, tan label, 1975....**10.00 - 20.00**

❑ RCA Victor LSP-2011(e), stereo, black label,
   dog near top, "Victor" at left, 1977 ....**6.00 - 12.00**

❑ RCA Victor AFL1-2011(e), stereo, black label,
   dog near top, "Victor" at left; includes copies
   with sticker wrapped around spine with new number,
   1977...**6.00 - 12.00**

Double Dynamite

❑ Pickwick DL2-5001, two-record set, 1975 ....**12.50 - 25.00**

❑ Pair PDL2-1010, two-record set, 1982 ....**10.00 - 20.00**

Double Trouble

❑ RCA Victor LPM-3787, mono, "Monaural" on label, with
bonus photo announcement on cover, 1967......**30.00 - 60.00**

❑ RCA Victor LSP-3787, stereo, "Stereo" on black label,
with bonus photo announcement on cover,
1967..**30.00 - 60.00**

❑ RCA Victor LPM/LSP-3787, bonus photo with either of above,
1967..**25.00 - 50.00**

❑ RCA Victor LPM-3787, mono, "Monaural" on label, with no
bonus photo announcement on cover, 1967......**40.00 - 80.00**

❑ RCA Victor LSP-3787, stereo, "Stereo" on black label, with no
bonus photo announcement on cover, 1967......**35.00 - 70.00**

❑ RCA Victor LSP-3787, stereo, orange label,
non-flexible vinyl, 1968 ....**20.00 - 40.00**

❑ RCA Victor LSP-3787, stereo, tan label, 1975........**10.00 - 20.00**

❑ RCA Victor LSP-3787, stereo, black label, dog near top,
"Victor" at left, 1977 ....**6.00 - 12.00**

❑ RCA Victor APL1-2564, stereo, black label, dog near top, "Victor"
at left; includes copies with sticker wrapped around spine with
"AFL1-2564" number, 1977..........................**6.00 - 12.00**

Early Elvis (1954-1956 Live at the Louisiana Hayride)

❑ Premore PL-589, 1989 ....**15.00 - 30.00**

Elvis

❑ RCA Victor LPM-1382, mono, with tracks listed on labels
as "Band 1" through "Band 6," back cover has ads for
other albums; 11 variations are known, each of
equal value, 1956.................................**200.00 - 400.00**

❑ RCA Victor LPM-1382, mono, with tracks listed on labels as "1"
through "6," back cover has ads for other albums; 11 variations
are known, each of equal value., 1956 .... **150.00 - 300.00**

❑ RCA Victor LPM-1382, mono, "Long Play" on label, back cover
has no ads for other albums, 1956 .... **150.00 - 300.00**

❑ RCA Victor LPM-1382, mono, with alternate take of
"Old Shep" on side 2, song 2; number in trail-off wax on
Side 2 ends in "15S," "17S" or "19S," but should be
played for positive ID; two lyric differences between the
standard and alternate takes are "Old Shep he grew old
AND his eyes were growing dim" (no AND on standard
version) and "And HE laid his old head on my knee"
(no HE on standard version), 1956 .... **400.00 - 800.00**

❑ RCA Victor LSP-1382(e), stereo, "Stereo Electronically
Reprocessed" and silver "RCA Victor" on label,
1962 .... **100.00 - 200.00**

❑ RCA Victor LPM-1382, mono, "Mono" on label,
1963 .... **40.00 - 80.00**

❑ RCA Victor LSP-1382(e), stereo, "Stereo" and white
"RCA Victor" on label, 1964 .... **25.00 - 50.00**

❑ RCA Victor LPM-1382, mono, "Monaural" on label,
1965 .... **30.00 - 60.00**

❑ RCA Victor LSP-1382(e), stereo, orange label,
  non-flexible vinyl, 1968 ....**15.00 - 30.00**

❑ RCA Victor LSP-1382(e), stereo, orange label,
  flexible vinyl, 1971 ....**10.00 - 20.00**

❑ RCA Victor LSP-1382(e), stereo, tan label, 1975 ..... **7.50 - 15.00**

❑ RCA Victor LSP-1382(e), stereo, black label,
  dog near top, 1976 ....**6.00 - 12.00**

❑ RCA Victor AFL1-1382(e), stereo, black label, dog near top,
  "Victor" at left; includes copies with sticker wrapped around
  spine with new number, 1977 ....**6.00 - 12.00**

❑ RCA Victor AFM1-5199, mono, 50th Anniversary reissue
  with banner, 1984 ....**10.00 - 20.00**

❑ RCA Victor LPM-1382, mono, red vinyl, "DRC 13271" in trail-off
  wax, "BMG Special Products" logo on back cover, from box
  "Elvis Top Album Collection Volume 1," 2003.....**10.00 - 20.00**

Elvis

Reissued as ELVIS COMMEMORATIVE ALBUM.

❑ RCA Special Products DPL2-0056(e), two-record set, mustard
  labels, "Brookville Records" on cover, 1973 ....**25.00 - 50.00**

❑ RCA Special Products DPL2-0056(e), two-record set, blue labels,
  1973..**12.50 - 25.00**

Elvis

including fool, it's impossible, where dO I GO FROM HERE, I'LL TAKE
YOU HOME AGAIN KATHLEEN, AND OTHERS

❑ RCA Victor APL1-0283, 1973............................**25.00 - 50.00**

Elvis (NBC-TV Special)

❑ RCA Victor LPM-4088, orange label, non-flexible vinyl,
   1968..**20.00 - 40.00**

❑ RCA Victor LPM-4088, orange label, flexible vinyl,
   1971..**15.00 - 30.00**

❑ RCA Victor LPM-4088, tan label, 1975...............**10.00 - 20.00**

❑ RCA Victor LPM-4088, black label, dog near top,
   "Victor" at left, 1976 ....**7.50 - 15.00**

❑ RCA Victor AFM1-4088, black label, dog near top, "Victor"
   at left; includes copies with sticker wrapped around spine
   with new number, 1977 ....**6.00 - 12.00**

❑ RCA Victor AYM1-3894, black label, dog near top, "Victor"
   at left, 1981..**4.00 - 8.00**

Elvis (One Night with You)

❑ RCA Special Products DVM1-0704, with poster (deduct 25% if
   missing), 1984 ....**30.00 - 60.00**

Elvis (Speaks to You)

❑ Green Valley GV-2001/3, two-record set, includes Elvis interviews plus tracks by the Jordanaires, 1978 ....**15.00 - 30.00**

Elvis Aron Presley

❑ RCA Victor CPL8-3699, eight-record box set, regular issue with booklet, 1980 ....**50.00 - 100.00**

❑ RCA Victor CPL8-3699, eight-record box set, with sticker on front idenitfying the copy as "Reviewer Series," 1980**125.00 - 250.00**

Elvis Aron Presley (Excerpts)

❑ RCA Victor DJL1-3729, promo only, excerpts of 37 songs from box set, 1980..**60.00 - 120.00**

Elvis Aron Presley (Selections)

❑ RCA Victor DJL1-3781, promo only, complete versions of 12 songs from box set, 1980...................................**60.00 - 120.00**

Elvis Aron Presley Forever

❑ Pair PDL2-1185, two-record set, 1988.............**10.00 - 20.00**

Elvis As Recorded at Madison Square Garden

❑ RCA Victor LSP-4776, orange label, 1972............**15.00 - 30.00**

❑ RCA Victor LSP-4776, orange label; with white timing sticker on front cover; counterfeit stickers have "Love Me" spelled as "Live Me," 1972 ....**50.00 - 100.00**

❑ RCA Victor SPS-33-571, two-record set, promo-only "Radio Station Banded Special Version"; came in plain white cover with stickers, 1972.............................**150.00 - 300.00**

❑ RCA Victor LSP-4776, tan label, 1975................**10.00 - 20.00**

❑ RCA Victor LSP-4776, black label, dog near top, "Victor" at left, 1976...**7.50 - 15.00**

❑ RCA Victor AFL1-4776, black label, dog near top, "Victor" at left; includes copies with sticker wrapped around spine with new number, 1977 ....**6.00 - 12.00**

❑ RCA Victor AQL1-4776, black label, dog near top, "Victor" at left, 1980 ....**4.00 - 8.00**

ELVIS AT SUN

❑ Sun/BMG 82876-61205-1, 2004 ....**7.50 - 15.00**

Elvis Commemorative Album

❏ RCA Special Products DPL2-0056(e), two-record set,
black label, dog near top, gold vinyl; reissue of Elvis
(same number), 1978 ....**40.00 - 80.00**

Elvis Country

❏ RCA Special Products DPL1-0647, 1984...............**15.00 - 30.00**

Elvis Country ("I'm 10,000 Years Old")

❏ RCA Victor LSP-4460, orange label, non-flexible vinyl,
1971..**20.00 - 40.00**

❏ RCA Victor LSP-4460, orange label, flexible vinyl,
1971..**12.50 - 25.00**

❏ RCA Victor LSP-4460, bonus photo, available in both
orange-label pressings, 1971 ....**7.50 - 15.00**

❏ RCA Victor LSP-4460, tan label, 1975.................**12.50 - 25.00**

❏ RCA Victor LSP-4460, black label, dog near top, "Victor"
at left, 1976..**7.50 - 15.00**

❏ RCA Victor LSP-4460, green vinyl; experimental pressing; black
label, dog near top, "Victor" at left, 1977 ....**1,000 – 2,000**

❑ RCA Victor AFL1-4460, black label, dog near top, "Victor" at left; includes copies with sticker wrapped around spine with new number, 1977 ....**6.00 - 12.00**

❑ RCA Victor AYL1-3956, black label, dog near top, "Victor" at left, 1981..**4.00 - 8.00**

Elvis Exclusive Live Press Conference (Memphis, Tennessee, February 1961)

❑ Green Valley GV-2001, flimsy, import-style cover; black stripe at top of back cover does NOT wrap around the spine, 1977 ....**20.00 - 40.00**

❑ Green Valley GV-2001, sturdier cpver; black stripe at top of back cover DOES wrap around the spine, 1977.........**15.00 - 30.00**

Elvis for Everyone

❑ RCA Victor LPM-3450, mono, "Monaural" on label, 1965..**30.00 - 60.00**

❑ RCA Victor LSP-3450, stereo, black label, dog on top, "Stereo" on label, 1965................................**30.00 - 60.00**

❑ RCA Victor LSP-3450, stereo, orange label, non-flexible vinyl, 1968...**20.00 - 40.00**

❑ RCA Victor LSP-3450, stereo, orange label, flexible vinyl, 1971 ....**10.00 - 20.00**

❑ RCA Victor LSP-3450, stereo, tan label, 1975 ....**10.00 - 20.00**

❑ RCA Victor LSP-3450, stereo, black label, dog near top, "Victor" at left, 1976 ....**6.00 - 12.00**

❑ RCA Victor AFL1-3450, stereo, black label, dog near top, "Victor" at left; includes copies with sticker wrapped around spine with new number, 1977 ....**6.00 - 12.00**

❑ RCA Victor AYL1-4232, stereo, black label, dog near top, "Victor" at left, 1982 ....**4.00 - 8.00**

Elvis Gospel 1957-1971 (Known Only to Him)

❑ RCA 9586-1-R, 1989 ....**20.00 - 40.00**

Elvis in Concert

❑ RCA Victor AFL2-2587, two-record set, both records on translucent blue vinyl; possibly an in-house demo at the RCA Indianapolis pressing plant, 1977 ....**500.00 – 1,000**

❑ RCA Victor APL2-2587, two-record set, custom labels, includes four-page brochure from Boxcar (dedcut 20% if missing), 1977 ....**12.50 - 25.00**

❑ RCA Victor CPL2-2587, two-record set, black labels,
    dog near top, "Victor" at left, new prefix, 1982....**20.00 - 40.00**

❑ RCA Victor APL2-2587, two-record set, red vinyl,
    "DRL 13360" in trail-off wax, "This is a replica of the
    original packaging" on back cover and all inserts;
    "DRL-23360" on back cover, from box "Elvis Top Album
    Collection Volume 1," 2003............................**10.00 - 20.00**

Elvis in Hollywood

❑ RCA Special Products DPL2-0168, two-record set, blue labels;
    with 20-page booklet, 1976............................**30.00 - 60.00**

Elvis in Nashville (1956-1971)

❑ RCA 8468-1-R, black label, dog near top, "Victor"
    at left, 1988...**20.00 - 40.00**

❑ RCA 8468-1-R, red label, 1988......................**12.50 - 25.00**

Elvis in Person at the International Hotel, Las Vegas, Nevada

❑ RCA Victor LSP-4428, orange label, non-flexible vinyl,
    1970...**25.00 - 50.00**

❑ RCA Victor LSP-4428, orange label, flexible vinyl,
   1971..**20.00 - 40.00**

❑ RCA Victor LSP-4428, tan label, 1975................**12.50 - 25.00**

❑ RCA Victor LSP-4428, black label, dog near top,
   "Victor" at left, 1976 ....**7.50 - 15.00**

❑ RCA Victor AFL1-4428, black label, dog near top;
   includes copies with sticker wrapped around spine
   with new number, 1977 ....**6.00 - 12.00**

❑ RCA Victor AYL1-3892, black label, dog near top,
   "Victor" at left, 1981 ....**4.00 - 8.00**

Elvis Is Back!

❑ RCA Victor LPM-2231, mono, "Long Play" on label,
   gatefold cover with slot for record behind front cover slick;
   no sticker attached to front cover; Side 2, Song 4 is listed
   as "The Girl Next Door," 1960...................**100.00 - 200.00**

❑ RCA Victor LPM-2231, mono, "Long Play" on label, gatefold
   cover with slot for record behind front cover slick; no sticker
   attached to front cover; Side 2, Song 4 is listed as "Girl Next
   Door Went a-Walking," 1960 ....**100.00 - 200.00**

❑ RCA Victor LPM-2231, mono, "Long Play" on label, gatefold cover with slot for record behind front cover slick; with sticker attached to front cover; Side 2, Song 4 is listed as "The Girl Next Door," 1960 ....**75.00 - 150.00**

❑ RCA Victor LPM-2231, mono, "Long Play" on label, gatefold cover with slot for record behind front cover slick; with sticker attached to front cover, Side 2, Song 4 is listed as "Girl Next Door Went a-Walking," 1960 ....**75.00 - 150.00**

❑ RCA Victor LSP-2231, stereo, "Living Stereo" on label, gatefold cover with slot for record behind front cover slick; no sticker attached to front cover; Side 2, Song 4 is listed as "The Girl Next Door," 1960 ....**150.00 - 300.00**

❑ RCA Victor LSP-2231, stereo, "Living Stereo" on label, gatefold cover with slot for record behind front cover slick; no sticker attached to front cover; Side 2, Song 4 is listed as "Girl Next Door Went a-Walking," 1960 ....**150.00 - 300.00**

❑ RCA Victor LSP-2231, stereo, "Living Stereo" on label; gatefold cover with slot for record behind front cover slick; with sticker attached to front cover; Side 2, Song 4 is listed as "The Girl Next Door," 1960 ....**150.00 - 300.00**

❑ RCA Victor LSP-2231, stereo, "Living Stereo" on label; gatefold cover with slot for record behind front cover slick; with sticker attached to front cover; Side 2, Song 4 is listed as "Girl Next Door Went a-Walking," 1960 ....**150.00 - 300.00**

❑ RCA Victor LPM-2231, mono, "Mono" on label; gatefold cover with slot for record behind back cover slick; song titles printed on front cover, 1963 ....**30.00 - 60.00**

❑ RCA Victor LPM-2231, mono, "Monaural" on label; gatefold cover with slot for record behind back cover slick; song titles printed on front cover, 1964 ....**30.00 - 60.00**

❑ RCA Victor LSP-2231, stereo, "Stereo" on bottom of label; gatefold cover with slot for record behind back cover slick; song titles printed on front cover, 1964 ....**30.00 - 60.00**

❑ RCA Victor LSP-2231, stereo, orange label, non-flexible vinyl, 1968 ....**20.00 - 40.00**

❑ RCA Victor LSP-2231, stereo, tan label, 1975 ....**10.00 - 20.00**

❑ RCA Victor LSP-2231, stereo, black label, dog near top, "Victor" at left; by this time, the cover is no longer a gatefold, 1976 ....**7.50 - 15.00**

❑ RCA Victor AFL1-2231, stereo, black label, dog near top, "Victor" at left; includes copies with sticker wrapped around spine with new number, 1977 ....**6.00 - 12.00**

❑ DCC Compact Classics LPZ-2037, stereo, white label, audiophile vinyl, gatefold cover restored, 1997................**60.00 - 120.00**

The Elvis Medley

❑ RCA Victor AHL1-4530, black label, dog near top, "Victor" at left, 1982 .... **6.00 - 12.00**

Elvis Now

❑ RCA Victor LSP-4671, orange label, 1972 .... **15.00 - 30.00**

❑ RCA Victor LSP-4671, promo, orange label; with white timing sticker on front cover, 1972 .... **50.00 - 100.00**

❑ RCA Victor LSP-4671, tan label, 1975 .... **12.50 - 25.00**

❑ RCA Victor LSP-4671, black label, dog near top, "Victor" at left, 1976 .... **7.50 - 15.00**

❑ RCA Victor AFL1-4671, black label, dog near top, "Victor" at left; includes copies with sticker wrapped around spine with new number, 1977 .... **6.00 - 12.00**

Elvis Presley

❑ RCA Victor LPM-1254, mono, Version 1: "Long Play" on label; "Elvis" in pale pink, "Presley" in pale green on cover; pale green and pale pink logo box in upper right front cover, 1956 .... **250.00 - 500.00**

❑ RCA Victor LPM-1254, mono, Version 2: "Long Play" on label; "Elvis" in pale pink, "Presley" in neon green on cover; neon green and pale pink logo box in upper right front cover, 1956 .... **200.00 - 400.00**

❑ RCA Victor LPM-1254, mono, Version 3: "Long Play" on label; "Elvis" in pale pink, "Presley" in neon green on cover; white bordered logo box in upper right front cover, "LPM-1254" in green at lower left, 1962 .... **125.00 - 250.00**

❑ RCA Victor LPM-1254, mono, Version 4: "Long Play" on label; "Elvis" in neon pink, almost red, "Presley" in neon green on cover; white bordered logo box in upper right front cover, "LPM-1254" in green at lower left, 1962 .... **100.00 - 200.00**

❑ RCA Victor LSP-1254(e), stereo, "Stereo Electronically Reprocessed" and silver "RCA Victor" on label, "Stereo Electronically Reprocessed" in pink at upper right front cover, 1962 .... **100.00 - 200.00**

❑ RCA Victor LPM-1254, mono, "Mono" on label; cover matches that on Version 4 above, 1963 .... **60.00 - 120.00**

❑ RCA Victor LPM-1254, mono, "Monaural" on label, cover matches that on Version 4 above, 1964 .... **30.00 - 60.00**

❑ RCA Victor LSP-1254(e), stereo, "Stereo" at bottom of label, white "RCA Victor" above dog at top of label, 1965 ...... **20.00 - 40.00**

❑ RCA Victor LSP-1254(e), stereo, orange label, non-flexible vinyl, "Victor" and "Stereo effect reproduced from monophonic" on upper right front cover, 1968 .... **15.00 - 30.00**

❑ RCA Victor LSP-1254(e), stereo, tan label, same front cover as orange label version, 1975 .... **7.50 - 15.00**

❑ RCA Victor LSP-1254(e), stereo, black label, dog near top, "Victor" at left, 1976 .... **6.00 - 12.00**

❑ RCA Victor AFL1-1254(e), stereo, black label, dog near top, "Victor" at left; includes copies with sticker wrapped around spine with new number, 1977 .... **6.00 - 12.00**

❑ RCA Victor AFM1-5198, mono, "Elvis 50th Anniversary" label, with banner, 1984 .... **10.00 - 20.00**

❑ RCA Victor LPM-1254, mono, red vinyl, "DRL 13272" in trail-off wax, "BMG Special Products" logo on back cover, from box "Elvis Top Album Collection Volume 1," 2003 .... **10.00 - 20.00**

The Elvis Presley Collection

❑ RCA Special Products DML3-0632, three-record boxed set, available through Candelite Music via mail order, 1984 .... **40.00 - 80.00**

Elvis Presley Interview Record:
An Audio Self-Portrait

❏ RCA Victor DJM1-0835, promotional item for "50th Anniversary"
series; later issued as RCA 6313-1-R, 1984........**40.00 - 80.00**

The Elvis PRESLEY Story

❏ RCA Special Products DML5-0263, five-record boxed set, available
through Candelite Music via mail order, 1977 ....**30.00 - 60.00**

Elvis Presley: 1954-1961

❏ Time-Life STL-106, 2-record box set, with insert of liner notes; part
of Time-Life's The Rock 'n' Roll Era series, 1986 ..... 15.00 - 30.00

Elvis Recorded Live on Stage in Memphis

❏ RCA Victor APD1-0606, quadraphonic, "RCA QuadraDisc"
labels and cover, 1974 ....**100.00 - 200.00**

❏ RCA Victor CPL1-0606, orange label, 1974 ....**12.50 - 25.00**

❏ RCA Victor DJL1-0606, orange label promo, special banded
version for radio airplay, 1974 ....**150.00 - 300.00**

❏ RCA Victor CPL1-0606, tan label, 1975...............**12.50 - 25.00**

❏ RCA Victor AFL1-0606, black label, dog near top, "Victor" at left; includes copies with sticker wrapped around spine with new number, 1977 .... 6.00 - 12.00

❏ RCA Victor AQL1-4776, black label, dog near top, "Victor" at left; 1979 .... 6.00 - 12.00

Elvis Sings Country Favorites

❏ Reader's Digest RDA-242/D, 1984 .... 30.00 - 60.00

Elvis Sings Flaming Star

❏ RCA Camden CAS-2304, blue label, non-flexible vinyl, 1969 .... 20.00 - 40.00

❏ RCA Camden CAS-2304, blue label, flexible vinyl, 1970 .... 15.00 - 30.00

❏ Pickwick CAS-2304, 1976 .... 5.00 - 10.00

Elvis Sings for Children and Grownups Too!

❏ RCA Victor CPL1-2901, black label, dog near top, "Victor" at left; gatefold cover; back cover has two slits for removable greeting card on back cover; deduct 20% if card is missing, 1978 .... 12.50 - 25.00

❑ RCA Victor CPL1-2901, black label, dog near top, "Victor" at left;
  gatefold cover; with greeting card graphic printed on back cover
  card, and no slits on back cover, 1981 .... **6.00 - 12.00**

❑ RCA Victor CPL1-2901, black label, dog near top, "Victor"
  at left; regular cover, 1981 .... **5.00 - 10.00**

Elvis Sings Hits from His Movies, Volume 1

❑ RCA Camden CAS-2567, 1972 .... **10.00 - 20.00**

❑ Pickwick CAS-2567, 1975 .... **5.00 - 10.00**

Elvis Sings Inspirational Favorites

❑ Reader's Digest RD4A-181/D, 1983 .... **10.00 - 20.00**

Elvis Sings the Wonderful World of Christmas

❑ RCA Victor LSP-4579, orange label; came with postcard,
  priced separately, 1971 .... **15.00 - 30.00**

❑ RCA Victor LSP-4579, postcard with above album, 1971,
  add this to above .... **10.00 - 20.00**

❑ RCA Victor ANL1-1936, orange label, 1975 .... **7.50 - 15.00**

❑ RCA Victor ANL1-1936, tan label, 1976 .... **6.00 - 12.00**

❑ RCA Victor ANL1-1936, black label, dog near top, "Victor" at left,
  1977 .... **5.00 - 10.00**

Elvis Talks!

❏ RCA 6313-1-R, 1987 .... **15.00 - 30.00**

The Elvis Tapes

❏ Great Northwest GNW-4005, 1977 .... **6.00 - 12.00**

Elvis the King: 1954-1965

❏ Time-Life STL-126, 2-record box set, with insert of liner notes; part of Time-Life's The Rock 'n' Roll Era series, 1989 ..... 40.00 - 80.00

Elvis Today

❏ RCA Victor APD1-1039, quadraphonic, "RCA QuadraDisc" labels and cover, 1975 .... **100.00 - 200.00**

❏ RCA Victor APL1-1039, stereo, orange label, 1975 . **30.00 - 60.00**

❏ RCA Victor APL1-1039, stereo, tan label, 1975 ...... **15.00 - 30.00**

❏ RCA Victor AFL1-1039, stereo, black label, dog near top, "Victor" at left; includes copies with sticker wrapped around spine with new number, 1977 .... **6.00 - 12.00**

❏ RCA Victor APD1-1039, quadraphonic, black label, dog near top; "RCA QuadraDisc" on cover, 1977 .... **75.00 - 150.00**

Elvis TOP ALBUM COLLECTION VOLUME 1

❑ Collectables COL-0165, contains reproductions, on red vinyl, of
five RCA albums (LPM-1254, LPM-1382, LSP-2370, LSP-2426
and APL2-2587) using facsimiles of original labels, covers,
inner sleeves and inserts; with poster and all in wooden box,
2003...**50.00 - 100.00**

Elvis TOP ALBUM COLLECTION VOLUME 2

❑ Collectables COL-0166, contains reproductions, on red vinyl, of
five RCA albums (LPM-1515, LOC-1035, LSP-2256, LSP-2999
and CPL2-2642) using facsimiles of original labels, covers,
inner sleeves and inserts; with poster and all in wooden box,
2003...**50.00 - 100.00**

Elvis' Christmas Album

❑ RCA Victor LOC-1035, mono, gatefold cover; title printed in gold
on LP spine; includes bound-in booklet, 1957 **250.00 - 500.00**

❑ RCA Victor LOC-1035, mono, gatefold cover; title printed in silver
on LP spine; includes bound-in booklet, 1957 **300.00 - 600.00**

❑ RCA Victor LOC-1035, mono, red vinyl; master number is
stamped in the trail-off wax; not to be confused
with the 2003 reissue in red vinyl, as only one copy is
known to exist, 1957...............................**10,000 – 15,000**

❑ RCA Victor LOC-1035, gold sticker with "To_____" and
"From_____" blanks and "ELVIS SINGS" below them,
1957, add to above .... **150.00 - 300.00**

❑ RCA Victor LPM-1951, mono, same album as LOC-1035,
but with a non-gatefold blue cover; "Long Play"
at bottom of label, 1958 .... **75.00 - 150.00**

❑ RCA Victor LPM-1951, mono, "Mono" at bottom of label:
"RE" on lower left front cover (photos on back were
altered), 1963 .... **35.00 - 70.00**

❑ RCA Victor LPM-1951, mono, "Monaural" at bottom of label;
"RE" on lower left front cover, 1964 .... **20.00 - 40.00**

❑ RCA Victor LSP-1951(e), stereo, black label, dog on top;
"Stereo" at bottom of label and "Stereo Electronically
Reproduced" on top of front cover, 1964 .... **25.00 - 50.00**

❑ RCA Victor LSP-1951(e), stereo, orange label, non-flexible
vinyl, "Stereo Effect Reprocessed from Mono" sticker on
cover, 1968 .... **30.00 - 60.00**

❑ RCA Camden CAL-2428, mono, reissue of LPM-1951 with two
songs added and four deleted; blue label, non-flexible vinyl,
1970 .... **15.00 - 30.00**

❑ RCA Camden CAL-2428, mono, blue label, flexible vinyl,
1971 .... **6.00 - 12.00**

❏ Pickwick CAS-2428, mono, "Pickwick" at upper left of front
cover; no Christmas trim around border of back cover,
1975...**5.00 - 10.00**

❏ Pickwick CAS-2428, mono, "Pickwick" at upper left of front
cover, with Christmas trim around border of back cover;
1976...**4.00 - 8.00**

❏ Pickwick CAS-2428, mono, "Pickwick" at upper left of
front cover, all print on back cover is in green ink;
1976...**12.50 - 25.00**

❏ RCA Victor AFM1-5486, mono, similar in design to
LOC-1035, though front cover is slightly different;
green vinyl with booklet, 1985 ....**10.00 - 20.00**

❏ RCA Victor AFM1-5486, mono, similar in design to LOC-1035,
though front cover is slightly different; black vinyl
with booklet, 1985...**7.50 - 15.00**

❏ RCA Special Products CAL-2428, mono, reissue for
"The Special Music Company," 1986.............**15.00 - 30.00**

❏ RCA Victor LOC-1035, mono, red vinyl, not to be mistaken
for the unique 1957 version, as this has a "DRL" number
in trail-off wax and "This is a replica of the original
packaging" on back cover; from box "Elvis Top Album
Collection Volume 2," 2003.........................**10.00 - 20.00**

Elvis' Gold Records Volume 2 — 50,000,000 Elvis Fans Can't Be Wrong

❑ RCA Victor LPM-2075, mono, "Long Play" on label; "Magic Millions" on upper right front cover with RCA Victor logo, 1960 .... **100.00 - 200.00**

❑ RCA Victor LSP-2075(e), stereo, "Stereo Electronically Reprocessed" on label; label has words "50,000,000 Elvis Presley Fans Can't Be Wrong," 1962 .... **75.00 - 150.00**

❑ RCA Victor LPM-2075, mono, "Mono" on label; "RE" on lower right front cover, 1963 .... **40.00 - 80.00**

❑ RCA Victor LPM-2075, mono, "Monaural" on label; label has words "50,000,000 Elvis Presley Fans Can't Be Wrong," 1964.. **25.00 - 50.00**

❑ RCA Victor LPM-2075, mono, "Monaural" on label; label has "Elvis' Gold Records - Vol. 2," without the reference to 50,000,000 fans, 1964.................................. **25.00 - 50.00**

❑ RCA Victor LSP-2075(e), stereo, "Stereo" on label; white "RCA Victor" at top above dog, 1964 .... **25.00 - 50.00**

❑ RCA Victor LSP-2075(e), stereo, orange label, non-flexible vinyl, 1968.. **15.00 - 30.00**

❑ RCA Victor LSP-2075(e), stereo, orange label, flexible vinyl, 1971.. **10.00 - 20.00**

❑ RCA Victor LSP-2075(e), sterep, tan label, 1975 ....**10.00 - 20.00**

❑ RCA Victor LSP-2075(e), stereo, black label, dog near top, "Victor" at left, 1976 .... **6.00 - 12.00**

❑ RCA Victor AFL1-2075(e), stereo, black label, dog near top, "Victor" at left; includes copies with sticker wrapped around spine with new number, 1977 .... **6.00 - 12.00**

❑ RCA Victor AFM1-5197, mono, 50th Anniversary
reissue in mono with banner, 1984 ....**10.00 - 20.00**

❑ RCA 07863-67643-1, mono, reissue for the Tower Records
chain with 10 bonus tracks, 1997 ....**15.00 - 30.00**

Elvis' Gold Records, Volume 4

❑ RCA Victor LPM-3921, mono, "Monaural"
on label, 1968...**1,500– 2,000**

❑ RCA Victor LSP-3921, stereo, "Stereo" and white
"RCA Victor" above dog on black label, 1968 ......**25.00 - 50.00**

❑ RCA Victor LSP-3921, stereo, orange label,
non-flexible vinyl, 1968 ....**20.00 - 40.00**

❑ RCA Victor LSP-3921, stereo, orange label,
flexible vinyl, 1970 ....**10.00 - 20.00**

❑ RCA Victor LSP-3921, stereo, tan label, 1975.......**12.50 - 25.00**

❑ RCA Victor LSP-3921, stereo, black label, dog near top,
"Victor" at left, 1976...................................**6.00 - 12.00**

❑ RCA Victor AFL1-3921, stereo, tan label
with new prefix, 1976...................................**7.50 - 15.00**

❑ RCA Victor AFL1-3921, stereo, black label, dog near top, "Victor"
at left; includes copies with sticker wrapped around spine with
new number, 1977.......................................**6.00 - 12.00**

Elvis' Gold Records, Volume 5

❑ RCA Victor AFL1-4941, 1984...........................**7.50 - 15.00**

Elvis' Golden Records

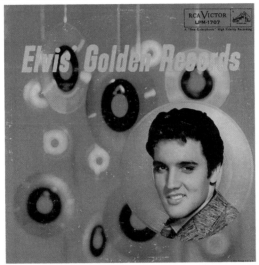

❑ RCA Victor LPM-1707, mono, title on cover in light blue letters;
no song titles listed on front cover, 1958 ...... **125.00 - 250.00**

❑ RCA Victor LPM-1707, mono, title on cover in light
blue letters; no song titles listed on front cover; "RE"
on back cover, 1958 ....**75.00 - 150.00**

❑ RCA Victor LSP-1707(e), stereo, "Stereo Electronically
Reprocessed" at bottom of label, silver "RCA Victor"
above dog on label, 1962 ....**100.00 - 200.00**

❑ RCA Victor LPM-1707, mono, "Mono" on label; title
on cover in white letters; song titles added to
front cover, 1963 ....**30.00 - 60.00**

❑ RCA Victor LPM-1707, mono, "Monaural" on label;
"RE2" on back cover, 1964 ....**20.00 - 40.00**

❑ RCA Victor LSP-1707(e), stereo, "Stereo" at bottom of label,
white "RCA Victor" above dog on label, 1964 ......**25.00 - 50.00**

❑ RCA Victor LSP-1707(e), stereo, orange label,
non-flexible vinyl, 1968 ....**15.00 - 30.00**

❑ RCA Victor LSP-1707(e), stereo, orange label, flexible vinyl,
1971 ....**10.00 - 20.00**

❑ RCA Victor LSP-1707(e), stereo, tan label, 1975 ....**10.00 - 20.00**

❑ RCA Victor LSP-1707(e), stereo, black label, dog near top,
"Victor" at left, 1976 ....**6.00 - 12.00**

❑ RCA Victor AFL1-1707(e), stereo, black label, dog near top,
"Victor" at left; includes copies with sticker wrapped
around spine with new number, 1977 ....**6.00 - 12.00**

❑ RCA Victor AQL1-1707(e), stereo, another reissue with
new prefix, 1979 ....**5.00 - 10.00**

❑ RCA Victor AFM1-5196, mono, 50th Anniversary reissue
in mono with banner, 1984..........................**10.00 - 20.00**

❑ RCA 07863-67642-1, mono, reissue for the
Tower Records chain with 6 bonus tracks, 1997 ..**15.00 - 30.00**

Elvis' Golden Records, Volume 3

❑ RCA Victor LPM-2765, mono, "Mono" on label,
1963..**50.00 - 100.00**

❑ RCA Victor LSP-2765, stereo, "Stereo" at bottom of label, silver
"RCA Victor" above dog on label, 1963 ....**75.00 - 150.00**

❑ RCA Victor LPM-2765, mono, "Monaural" on label,
1964..**30.00 - 60.00**

❑ RCA Victor LSP-2765, stereo, "Stereo" at bottom of label, white
"RCA Victor" above dog on label, 1964 ....**25.00 - 50.00**

❑ RCA Victor LSP-2765, stereo, orange label,
non-flexible vinyl, 1968 ....**20.00 - 40.00**

❑ RCA Victor LSP-2765, stereo, tan label, 1975........**10.00 - 20.00**

❑ RCA Victor LSP-2765, stereo, black label, dog near top,
"Victor" at left, 1976 ....**6.00 - 12.00**

❑ RCA Victor AFL1-2765, stereo, black label, dog near top, "Victor"
at left; includes copies with sticker wrapped around spine with
new number, 1977......................................**6.00 - 12.00**

Essential Elvis: The First Movies

❏ RCA 6738-1-R, 1988 .... **12.50 - 25.00**

Essential Elvis, Vol. 2 (Stereo '57)

❏ RCA 9589-1-R, 1989 .... **12.50 - 25.00**

50 Years — 50 Hits

❏ RCA Special Products SVL3-0710, three-record set,
1985 .... **15.00 - 30.00**

The First Live Recordings

❏ Music Works PB-3601, 1984 .... **7.50 - 15.00**

The First of Elvis

❏ Show-Land LP-2001, 1979 .... **50.00 - 100.00**

The First Year (Elvis, Scotty and Bill)

❏ Golden Editions KING-1, 1979 .... **7.50 - 15.00**

❏ Golden Editions GEL-101, 1979 .... **10.00 - 20.00**

The First Years

❏ HALW HALW-0001, With stamped, limited edition number,
1978 .... **15.00 - 30.00**

❑ HALW HALW-0001, Without limited edition number,
   1978..**10.00 - 20.00**

For LP Fans Only

❑ RCA Victor LPM-1990, mono, "Long Play"
   on label, 1959......................................**125.00 - 250.00**

❑ RCA Victor LPM-1990, mono, "Mono" on label, "RE"
   on cover, 1963.......................................**40.00 - 80.00**

❑ RCA Victor LPM-1990, mono, "Monaural" on label,
   1964...**25.00 - 50.00**

❑ RCA Victor LSP-1990(e), stereo, "Stereo" on label; with same
   photo on both front and back, 1965............**150.00 - 300.00**

❑ RCA Victor LSP-1990(e), stereo, "Stereo" on label; with
   different front and back cover photos, 1965.......**25.00 - 50.00**

❑ RCA Victor LSP-1990(e), stereo, orange label,
   non-flexible vinyl, 1968...............................**15.00 - 30.00**

❑ RCA Victor LSP-1990(e), stereo, tan label, 1975....**10.00 - 20.00**

❑ RCA Victor LSP-1990(e), stereo, black label, dog near top,
   "Victor" at left, 1976....................................**6.00 - 12.00**

❑ RCA Victor AFL1-1990(e), stereo, black label, dog near top;
   includes copies with sticker wrapped around spine with new
   number, 1977..**6.00 - 12.00**

Frankie and Johnny

❑ RCA Victor LPM-3553, mono, "Monaural" on label,
   1966..**30.00 - 60.00**

❑ RCA Victor LSP-3553, stereo, "Stereo" on black label,
   1966..**30.00 - 60.00**

❑ RCA Victor LPM/LSP-3553, bonus print of an Elvis portrait,
   1966, add this to above....................................**30.00 - 60.00**

❑ Pickwick ACL-7007, 1976 ....**5.00 - 10.00**

From Elvis in Memphis

❑ RCA Victor LSP-4155, orange label, non-flexible vinyl,
   1969..**20.00 - 40.00**

❑ RCA Victor LSP-4155, bonus photo, 1969,
   add to above...**20.00 - 40.00**

❑ RCA Victor LSP-4155, orange label, flexible vinyl,
   1971..**15.00 - 30.00**

❑ RCA Victor LSP-4155, tan label, 1975................**12.50 - 25.00**

❑ RCA Victor LSP-4155, black label, dog near top,
   1976..**7.50 - 15.00**

❑ RCA Victor AFL1-4155, black label, dog near top,
   "Victor" at left; includes copies with sticker wrapped
   around spine with new number, 1977 ....**6.00 - 12.00**

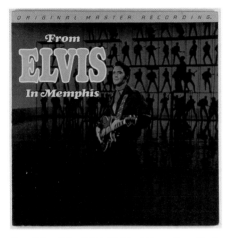

❏ Mobile Fidelity 1-059, "Original Master Recording" at top of
front cover, 1982...**25.00 - 50.00**

From Elvis Presley Boulevard, Memphis, Tennessee

❏ RCA Victor APL1-1506, tan label, 1976..............**15.00 - 30.00**

❏ RCA Victor AFL1-1506, black label, dog near top, "Victor" at left;
with sticker wrapped around spine with new number
(old number still on label), 1977......................**6.00 - 12.00**

❏ RCA Victor AFL1-1506, black label, dog near top, "Victor" at left; new number is on cover and label, 1977............**5.00 - 10.00**

From Elvis with Love

❏ RCA Victor R 234340, two-record set, RCA Music Service exclusive, 1978.................................**20.00 - 40.00**

From Memphis to Vegas/From Vegas to Memphis

❏ RCA Victor LSP-6020, two-record set, orange labels, non-flexible vinyl; with incorrect composers listed for "Words" (Tommy Boyce and Bobby Hart) and "Suspicious Minds" (Frances Zambon), 1969...................................**75.00 - 150.00**

❏ RCA Victor LSP-6020, two-record set, orange labels, non-flexible vinyl; with correct composers listed for "Words" (Barry, Robin and Maurice Gibb) and "Suspicious Minds" (Mark James), 1969.................................**50.00 - 100.00**

❏ RCA Victor LSP-6020, bonus photos; four different photos came with different copies of this LP, but no more than two per album; value is for any two different photos, 1969, add to above................................**25.00 - 50.00**

❏ RCA Victor LSP-6020, two-record set, orange labels, flexible vinyl, 1971 ....**20.00 - 40.00**

❏ RCA Victor LSP-6020, two-record set, tan labels, 1975..**15.00 - 30.00**

❑ RCA Victor LSP-6020, two-record set, black label, dog near top, "Victor" at left, 1976 ....**10.00 - 20.00**

Fun in Acapulco

❑ RCA Victor LPM-2756, mono, "Mono" on label, 1963..**40.00 - 80.00**

❑ RCA Victor LSP-2756, stereo, "Stereo" at bottom of label, silver "RCA Victor" at top above dog on label, 1963 ...**50.00 - 100.00**

❑ RCA Victor LPM-2756, mono, "Monaural" on label, 1964 ..**25.00 - 50.00**

❑ RCA Victor LSP-2756, stereo, "Stereo" at bottom of label, white "RCA Victor" at top above dog on label, 1964 .....**30.00 - 60.00**

❑ RCA Victor LSP-2756, stereo, orange label, non-flexible vinyl, 1968..**20.00 - 40.00**

❑ RCA Victor LSP-2756, stereo, tan label, 1975........**12.50 - 25.00**

❑ RCA Victor LSP-2756, stereo, black label, dog near top, "Victor" at left, 1976 ....**6.00 - 12.00**

❑ RCA Victor AFL1-2756, stereo, black label, dog near top, "Victor" at left; includes copies with sticker wrapped around spine with new number, 1977......................................**6.00 - 12.00**

G.I. Blues

❑ RCA Victor LPM-2256, mono, "Long Play" on label;
with sticker on front cover advertising the presence
of "Wooden Heart," 1960.......................**250.00 - 500.00**

❑ RCA Victor LPM-2256, mono, "Long Play" on label;
with no sticker on front cover, 1960..............**60.00 - 120.00**

❑ RCA Victor LSP-2256, stereo, "Living Stereo" on label;
with sticker on front cover advertising the presence of
"Wooden Heart," 1960............................**300.00 - 600.00**

❑ RCA Victor LSP-2256, stereo, "Living Stereo" on label;
with no sticker on front cover, 1960..............**50.00 - 100.00**

❑ RCA Victor LPM-2256, mono, "Mono" on label,
1963...**50.00 - 100.00**

❑ RCA Victor LPM-2256, mono, "Monaural" on label,
1964..**25.00 - 50.00**

❑ RCA Victor LSP-2256, stereo, "Stereo" on black label,
"RCA Victor" in white above dog, 1964.............**25.00 - 50.00**

❑ RCA Victor LSP-2256, stereo, orange label, non-flexible
vinyl, 1968.......................................**20.00 - 40.00**

❑ RCA Victor LSP-2256, stereo, orange label, flexible vinyl,
1971..**10.00 - 20.00**

❑ RCA Victor LSP-2256, stereo, tan label, 1975........**12.50 - 25.00**

❑ RCA Victor LSP-2256, stereo, black label, dog near top,
   "Victor" at left, 1976 ....**6.00 - 12.00**

❑ RCA Victor AFL1-2256, stereo, black label, dog near top, "Victor"
   at left; includes copies with sticker wrapped around spine with
   new number, 1977......................................**6.00 - 12.00**

❑ RCA Victor AYL1-3735, stereo, [black label, dog near top,
   "Victor" at left, 1980 ....**4.00 - 8.00**

❑ RCA Victor LSP-2256, stereo, red vinyl, "DRL" number in trail-
   off wax, "BMG Special Products" logo on back cover, from box
   "Elvis Top Album Collection Volume 2," 2003.....**10.00 - 20.00**

Girl Happy

❑ RCA Victor LPM-3338, mono, "Monaural" on label,
   1965...**30.00 - 60.00**

❑ RCA Victor LSP-3338, stereo, "Stereo" at bottom of label, "RCA
   Victor" in white above dog on label, 1965 ....**30.00 - 60.00**

❑ RCA Victor LSP-3338, stereo, orange label,
   non-flexible vinyl, 1968 ....**20.00 - 40.00**

❑ RCA Victor LSP-3338, stereo, orange label, flexible vinyl,
   1971...**10.00 - 20.00**

❑ RCA Victor LSP-3338, stereo, tan label, 1975........**12.50 - 25.00**

❑ RCA Victor LSP-3338, stereo, black label, dog near top,
"Victor" at left, 1976 ....**6.00 - 12.00**

❑ RCA Victor AFL1-3338, stereo, black label, dog near top, "Victor"
at left; includes copies with sticker wrapped around spine with
new number, 1977 ....**6.00 - 12.00**

Girls! Girls! Girls!

❑ RCA Victor LPM-2621, mono, "Long Play" on label,
1962 ....**40.00 - 80.00**

❑ RCA Victor LSP-2621, stereo, "Living Stereo" on label,
1962 ....**75.00 - 150.00**

❑ RCA Victor LPM/LSP-2621, bonus 1963 calendar with above
editions; has listing of other Elvis records on back; if something
else is on the back, it is *not* the version that came with this
album, 1962, add to above ....**75.00 - 150.00**

❑ RCA Victor LPM-2621, mono, "Mono" on label,
1963 ....**30.00 - 60.00**

❑ RCA Victor LPM-2621, mono, "Monaural" on label,
1964 ....**20.00 - 40.00**

❑ RCA Victor LSP-2621, stereo, "Stereo" at bottom of label, "RCA
Victor" in white above dog at top, 1964 ....**30.00 - 60.00**

❑ RCA Victor LSP-2621, stereo, orange label, non-flexible vinyl, 1968 ....**20.00 - 40.00**

❑ RCA Victor LSP-2621, stereo, orange label, flexible vinyl, 1971 ....**10.00 - 20.00**

❑ RCA Victor LSP-2621, stereo, tan label, 1975........**12.50 - 25.00**

❑ RCA Victor LSP-2621, stereo, black label, dog near top, "Victor" at left, 1976 ....**6.00 - 12.00**

❑ RCA Victor AFL1-2621, stereo, black label, dog near top, "Victor" at left; includes copies with sticker wrapped around spine with new number, 1977 ....**6.00 - 12.00**

A Golden Celebration

❑ RCA Victor CPM6-5172, six-record set, 1984 ......**50.00 - 100.00**

Good Rockin' Tonight

❑ RCA Special Products SVL2-0824, two-record set, 1988 ....**10.00 - 20.00**

Good Times

❑ RCA Victor CPL1-0475, orange label, 1974 ....**25.00 - 50.00**

❑ RCA Victor CPL1-0475, black label, dog near top, "Victor" at left, 1976 ....**6.00 - 12.00**

❑ RCA Victor AFL1-0475, black label, dog near top, "Victor" at left; includes copies with sticker wrapped around spine with new number, 1977 .... **6.00 - 12.00**

Great Hits of 1956-57

❑ Reader's Digest RBA-072/D, 1987 ....**10.00 - 20.00**

The Great Performances

❑ RCA 2227-1-R, 1990 ....**20.00 - 40.00**

Greatest Hits, Volume One

❑ RCA Victor AHL1-2347, with embossed cover, 1981..**12.50 - 25.00**

❑ RCA Victor AHL1-2347, without embossed cover, 1983..**7.50 - 15.00**

The Greatest Moments in Music

❑ RCA Special Products DML1-0413, 1980 ....**7.50 - 15.00**

The Greatest Show on Earth

❑ RCA Special Products DML1-0348, 1978 ....**7.50 - 15.00**

Guitar Man

❏ RCA Victor AAL1-3917, 1981.............................**15.00 - 30.00**

Harum Scarum

❏ RCA Victor LPM-3468, mono, "Monaural" on label,
1965..**30.00 - 60.00**

❏ RCA Victor LSP-3468, stereo, "Stereo" at bottom
of black label, 1965 ....**30.00 - 60.00**

❏ RCA Victor LPM/LSP-3468, bonus photo with
either version, 1965, add to above...................**30.00 - 60.00**

❏ RCA Victor APL1-2558, stereo, black label, dog near top,
"Victor" at left, 1977 ....**6.00 - 12.00**

❏ RCA Victor AYL1-3734, stereo, black label, dog near top,
"Victor" at left, 1980 ....**4.00 - 8.00**

Having Fun with Elvis on Stage

❏ Boxcar (no #), white label with black and orange print, "Boxcar"
logo at upper left of front cover, 1974 ....**75.00 - 150.00**

❏ RCA Victor CPM1-0818, commercial issue of Boxcar LP; orange
label, 1974...**15.00 - 30.00**

❏ RCA Victor CPM1-0818, tan label, 1975..............**10.00 - 20.00**

❏ RCA Victor AFM1-0818, black label, dog near top, "Victor" at left,
1977...**12.50 - 25.00**

He Touched Me

❑ RCA Victor LSP-4690, orange label, 1972............**20.00 - 40.00**

❑ RCA Victor LSP-4690, orange label promo; with white timing
sticker on front cover, 1972........................**50.00 - 100.00**

❑ RCA Victor LSP-4690, tan label, 1975................**10.00 - 20.00**

❑ RCA Victor LSP-4690, black label, dog near top, "Victor"
at left, 1976..**7.50 - 15.00**

❑ RCA Victor AFL1-4690, black label, dog near top, "Victor"
at left; includes copies with sticker wrapped around spine
with new number, 1977 ....**6.00 - 12.00**

He Walks Beside Me

❑ RCA Victor AFL1-2772, includes 20-page photo booklet,
1978...**12.50 - 25.00**

The Hillbilly Cat

❑ Music Works PB-3602, 1984............................**7.50 - 15.00**

His Greatest Hits

❑ Reader's Digest RD-10/A, eight-record set, white slipcover over
white case, "RD-10/A" is number on box; "RD4A-010 is number
on records," 1979...................................**200.00 - 400.00**

❏ Reader's Digest 010/A, seven-record set, yellow slipcover over
 white case, "010/A" is number on box, "RDA4-010" is number
 on records, 1983 ....**30.00 - 60.00**

❏ Reader's Digest 010/A, seven-record set, white slipcover over
 white case, "010/A" is number on box, "RDA4-010" is number
 on records, 1990 ....**20.00 - 40.00**

His Hand in Mine

❏ RCA Victor LPM-2328, mono, "Long Play" on label,
 1960.....................................**60.00 - 120.00**

❏ RCA Victor LSP-2328, stereo, "Living Stereo" on label,
 1960.....................................**100.00 - 200.00**

❏ RCA Victor LPM-2328, mono, "Mono" on label,
 1963.....................................**30.00 - 60.00**

❏ RCA Victor LSP-2328, stereo, "Stereo" at bottom of label,
 silver "RCA Victor" at top of black label above dog,
 1964.....................................**300.00 - 600.00**

❏ RCA Victor LPM-2328, mono, "Monaural" on label,
 1964.....................................**25.00 - 50.00**

❏ RCA Victor LSP-2328, stereo, "Stereo" at bottom of label,
 white "RCA Victor" at top of black label above dog,
 1964.....................................**50.00 - 100.00**

❑ RCA Victor LSP-2328, stereo, orange label,
   non-flexible vinyl, 1968 ....**25.00 - 50.00**

❑ RCA Victor LSP-2328, stereo, orange label,
   flexible vinyl, 1971 ....**10.00 - 20.00**

❑ RCA Victor LSP-2328, stereo, tan label, 1975.......**10.00 - 20.00**

❑ RCA ANL1-1319, stereo, orange label, no "Victor";
   reissue with more tightly cropped photo of Elvis on
   front cover, 1976......................................**7.50 - 15.00**

❑ RCA Victor AYL1-3935, stereo, yellow label; includes copies
   with sticker wrapped around spine with new number,
   1981..**4.00 - 8.00**

His Songs of Faith and Inspiration

❑ RCA Special Products DVL2-0728, two-record set,
   1986..**25.00 - 50.00**

His Songs of Inspiration

❑ RCA Special Products DML1-0264, 1977 ....**7.50 - 15.00**

How Great Thou Art

❑ RCA Victor LPM-3758, mono, "Mono Dynagroove"
   on label, 1967..**30.00 - 60.00**

❑ RCA Victor LSP-3758, stereo, "Stereo Dynagroove"
   on black label, 1967.................................**30.00 - 60.00**

❏ RCA Victor LSP-3758, stereo, orange label, non-flexible vinyl,
  1968..**20.00 - 40.00**

❏ RCA Victor LSP-3758, stereo, orange label, flexible vinyl,
  1971..**12.50 - 25.00**

❏ RCA Victor LSP-3758, stereo, tan label, 1975........**10.00 - 20.00**

❏ RCA Victor LSP-3758, stereo, black label, dog near top, "Victor" at
  left, 1976..**6.00 - 12.00**

❏ RCA Victor AFL1-3758, stereo, black label, dog near top, "Victor"
  at left; includes copies with sticker wrapped around spine with
  new number, 1977...**6.00 - 12.00**

❏ RCA Victor AQL1-3758, stereo, black label, dog near top, "Victor"
  at left; reissue with new prefix, 1979.................**5.00 - 10.00**

I Got Lucky

❏ RCA Camden CAL-2533, blue label, 1971............**12.50 - 25.00**

❏ Pickwick CAS-2533, black label, 1975.................**5.00 - 10.00**

I Was the One

❏ RCA Victor AHL1-4678, 1983............................**5.00 - 10.00**

International Hotel, Las Vegas Nevada, Presents Elvis, 1969

❑ RCA Victor (no #), gift box to guests at Elvis' July 31-Aug, 1, 1969 shows; includes LPM-4088 and LSP-4155; press release; 1969 catalog; three photos; and thank-you note from Elvis and the Colonel; most of the value is for the box, 1969…**1,750 – 2,500**

International Hotel, Las Vegas Nevada, Presents Elvis, 1970

❑ RCA Victor (no #), gift box to guests at Elvis' Jan. 28, 1970 show; includes LSP-6020 and 47-9791; press release; 1970 catalog; photo; booklet; and dinner menu; most of the value is for the box., 1970...**1,750 – 2,500**

Interviews with Elvis (Canada 1957)

❑ Gusto SD-995, reissue of Great Northwest album, 1978...**20.00 - 40.00**

It Happened at the World's Fair

❑ RCA Victor LPM-2697, mono, "Long Play" on label, 1963..**60.00 - 120.00**

❑ RCA Victor LSP-2697, stereo, "Living Stereo" and silver "RCA Victor" on black label, 1963 ....**100.00 - 200.00**

❏ RCA Victor LPM/LSP-2697, photo insert, three different poses on
one sheet; counterfeits have distorted colors and images, 1963,
add to above...**125.00 - 250.00**

❏ RCA Victor LSP-2697, stereo, "Stereo" at bottom of label,
white "RCA Victor" above dog at top of black label,
1964...**40.00 - 80.00**

❏ RCA Victor APL1-2568, stereo, black label, dog near top, "Victor"
at left, 1977...**6.00 - 12.00**

King Creole

❏ RCA Victor LPM-1884, mono, "Long Play" on label,
not officially released with a bonus photo, but see
next listing, 1958 ....**100.00 - 200.00**

❏ RCA Victor LPM-1884, "bonus photo"; an 8x10 black and white
photo of Elvis in his Army uniform signed "Best Wishes, Elvis
Presley," was NOT officially part of the LP package, though it
has been found inside a "sealed" copy of this LP; most likely,
the sealing was done by a record store, 1958 .. **100.00 - 200.00**

❏ RCA Victor LSP-1884(e), stereo, "Stereo Electronically
Reprocessed" and silver "RCA Victor" on label,
1962...**75.00 - 150.00**

❏ RCA Victor LPM-1884, mono, "Mono" on label,
1963...**40.00 - 80.00**

❏ RCA Victor LPM-1884, mono, "Monaural" on label,
1964...**30.00 - 60.00**

❑ RCA Victor LSP-1884(e), stereo, "Stereo" at bottom of
   label, white "RCA Victor" above dog on top of black label,
   1964 . . . .**30.00 - 60.00**

❑ RCA Victor LSP-1884(e), stereo, orange label, non-flexible
   vinyl, 1968 . . . .**20.00 - 40.00**

❑ RCA Victor LSP-1884(e), stereo, orange label, flexible vinyl,
   1971 . . . .**10.00 - 20.00**

❑ RCA Victor LSP-1884(e), stereo, tan label, 1975 . . . .**10.00 - 20.00**

❑ RCA Victor LSP-1884(e), stereo, black label, dog near top,
   "Victor" on left, 1976 . . . . **6.00 - 12.00**

❑ RCA Victor AFL1-1884(e), stereo, black label, dog near top,
   "Victor" on left; includes copies with sticker wrapped around
   spine with new number, 1977 . . . . **6.00 - 12.00**

❑ RCA Victor AYL1-3733, stereo, black label, dog near top, "Victor"
   on left; includes copies with sticker wrapped around spine with
   new number, 1980 . . . .**4.00 - 8.00**

The King Speaks (February 1961, Memphis, Tennessee)

❑ Great Northwest GV-2004, label says this is on "Green Valley"
   while sleeve says "Great Northwest," 1977 . . . . **5.00 - 10.00**

❑ Great Northwest GNW-4006, both label and sleeve say this is on
   "Great Northwest," 1977 . . . .**4.00 - 8.00**

Kissin' Cousins

❑ RCA Victor LPM-2894, mono, "Mono" on label; front
cover does NOT have black and white photo at lower
right, 1964 ....**100.00 - 200.00**

❑ RCA Victor LPM-2894, mono, "Mono" on label; front cover has a
small black and white photo of six cast members at lower right,
1964 ....**40.00 - 80.00**

❑ RCA Victor LSP-2894, stereo, "Stereo" at bottom of label,
silver "RCA Victor" above dog on top of black label;
front cover does NOT have black and white photo in
lower right, 1964 ....**100.00 - 200.00**

❑ RCA Victor LSP-2894, stereo, "Stereo" at bottom of label, silver
"RCA Victor" above dog on top of black label; front cover has a
small black and white photo of six cast members at lower right,
1964 ....**60.00 - 120.00**

❑ RCA Victor LPM-2894, mono, "Monaural" on label;
front cover does NOT have black and white photo at
lower right, 1964 ....**100.00 - 200.00**

❑ RCA Victor LPM-2894, mono, "Monaural" on label; front cover
has a small black and white photo of six cast members at lower
right, 1964 ....**50.00 - 100.00**

❑ RCA Victor LSP-2894, stereo, "Stereo" at bottom of label, white
"RCA Victor" above dog on top of black label; front cover has
the cast photo at lower right, 1964 ....**30.00 - 60.00**

❑ RCA Victor LSP-2894, stereo, orange label, non-flexible vinyl,
1968 ....**20.00 - 40.00**

❏ RCA Victor LSP-2894, stereo, orange label, flexible vinyl,
  1971..**10.00 - 20.00**

❏ RCA Victor LSP-2894, stereo, tan label, 1975.......**12.50 - 25.00**

❏ RCA Victor LSP-2894, stereo, black label, dog near top,
  "Victor" at left, 1976 .... **6.00 - 12.00**

❏ RCA Victor LSP-2894, stereo, black label, dog near top, "Victor" at
  left; experimental blue vinyl pressing, 1976 ... **750.00 – 1,500.**

❏ RCA Victor AFL1-2894, stereo, black label, dog near top, "Victor"
  at left; includes copies with sticker wrapped around spine with
  new number, 1977...................................... **6.00 - 12.00**

❏ RCA Victor AYL1-4115, stereo, black label, dog near top, "Victor"
  at left; includes copies with sticker wrapped around spine with
  new number, 1981......................................**4.00 - 8.00**

The Legend Lives On

❏ Reader's Digest RB4-191/A, seven-record set, number
  on box is "010/A" but records have "RB4-191" on them,
  1986...**30.00 - 60.00**

The Legendary Concert Performances

❏ RCA Victor R 244047, two-record set, RCA Music Service
  exclusive, 1978...**20.00 - 40.00**

The Legendary Magic of Elvis Presley

❏ RCA Special Products DVL1-0461, 1980................ **7.50 - 15.00**

A Legendary Performer, Volume 1

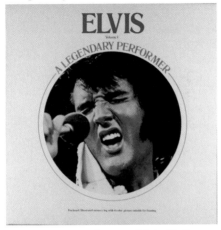

❑ RCA Victor CPL1-0341, custom label; with die-cut
hole in front cover; includes booklet (deduct 40% if missing),
1974 .... **12.50 - 25.00**

❑ RCA Victor CPL1-0341, promo-only experimental
picture disc; one uses the image from the *Elvis Presley* LP;
one uses the image from the Elvis LP; one uses the image
from the Elvis Now LP; others may exist; these were for
in-house use only and were not issued to the public; price
is for any of them, 1978 .... **1,000 – 2,000**

❑ RCA Victor CPL1-0341, no die-cut hole in cover and no booklet,
1986... **7.50 - 15.00**

A Legendary Performer, Volume 2

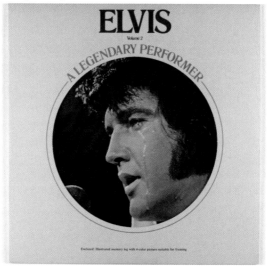

❑ RCA Victor CPL1-1349, custom label; with die-cut hole
in front cover; includes booklet (deduct 40% if missing),
1976...**15.00 - 30.00**

❑ RCA Victor CPL1-1349, custom label; Side 2 is missing
false starts and outtakes for the songs "Such a Night"
and "Cane and a High Starched Collar"; which are
supposed to be there; the end of of the number in the
trail-off wax is "31," 1976..............................**30.00 - 60.00**

❑ RCA Victor CPL1-1349, no die-cut hole in cover and
no booklet, 1986......................................**7.50 - 15.00**

A Legendary Performer, Volume 3

❑ RCA Victor CPL1-3078, picture disc applied to blue vinyl LP; with
die-cut hole in front cover; includes booklet (deduct 40% if
missing), 1978..**12.50 - 25.00**

❑ RCA Victor CPL1-3082, custom label; black vinyl; with die-cut
hole in front cover; includes booklet (deduct 40% if missing),
1978...**12.50 - 25.00**

❑ RCA Victor CPL1-3082, no die-cut hole in cover and no booklet,
1986..**4.00 - 8.00**

A Legendary Performer, Volume 4

❑ RCA Victor CPL1-4848, custom label; with die-cut hole
in back cover; includes booklet (deduct 40% if missing),
1983...**15.00 - 30.00**

❑ RCA Victor CPL1-4848, no die-cut hole in cover and no booklet,
1986...**10.00 - 20.00**

The Legendary Recordings of Elvis Presley

❏ RCA Special Products DML6-0412, six-record set,
1979...**50.00 - 100.00**

Let's Be Friends

❏ RCA Camden CAS-2408, blue label, 1970 ....**15.00 - 30.00**

❏ Pickwick CAS-2408, black label, 1975................**5.00 - 10.00**

❏ Pickwick CAS-2408, black label, gold or multi-color
vinyl, experimental pressings not offered to the public,
1977..**500.00 – 1,000**

Lightning Strikes Twice

❏ United Distributors UDL-2382, mono, Side 1 has five
Beatles' Decca audition tracks; Side 2 has live Elvis Presley
performances from 1955, 1981 ....**30.00 - 60.00**

Love Letters from Elvis

❏ RCA Victor LSP-4530, orange label; "Love Letters from"
on one line of front cover, "Elvis" on a second line,
1971..**20.00 - 40.00**

❏ RCA Victor LSP-4530, orange label; "Love Letters" on one line
of front cover; "from" on a second line, "Elvis" on a third line,
1971..**15.00 - 30.00**

❏ RCA Victor LSP-4530, tan label; "Love Letters from" on one line
of front cover, "Elvis" on a second line, 1975 .....**15.00 - 30.00**

❑ RCA Victor LSP-4530, tan label; "Love Letters" on one line of front cover; "from" on a second line, "Elvis" on a third line, 1975..**12.50 - 25.00**

❑ RCA Victor LSP-4530, black label, dog near top, "Victor" at left, 1976..**10.00 - 20.00**

❑ RCA Victor AFL1-4530, Black label, dog near top. "Victor" at left; includes copies with sticker wrapped around spine with new number, 1977 ....**6.00 - 12.00**

Love Songs

❑ K-Tel NU 9900, 1981...................................**10.00 - 20.00**

Loving You

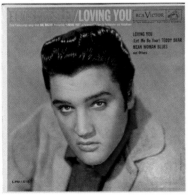

❑ RCA Victor LPM-1515, mono, "Long Play" on label,
1957...**150.00 - 300.00**

❑ RCA Victor LSP-1515(e), stereo, "Stereo Electronically
Reprocessed" and silver "RCA Victor" on label,
1962...**75.00 - 150.00**

❑ RCA Victor LPM-1515, mono, "Mono" on label,
1963...**50.00 - 100.00**

❑ RCA Victor LPM-1515, mono, "Monaural" on label,
1964...**25.00 - 50.00**

❑ RCA Victor LSP-1515(e), stereo, " Stereo" at bottom
of label, white "RCA Victor" above dog on black label,
1964...**25.00 - 50.00**

❑ RCA Victor LSP-1515(e), stereo, orange label,
non-flexible vinyl, 1968 ....**20.00 - 40.00**

❑ RCA Victor LSP-1515(e), stereo, orange label, flexible vinyl,
1971...**10.00 - 20.00**

❑ RCA Victor LSP-1515(e), stereo, tan label, 1975....**10.00 - 20.00**

❑ RCA Victor LSP-1515(e), stereo, black label, dog near top,
"Victor" at left, 1976 ....**6.00 - 12.00**

❑ RCA Victor AFL1-1515(e), stereo, black label, dog near top,
"Victor" at left; includes copies with sticker wrapped around
spine with new number, 1977 ....**6.00 - 12.00**

❑ RCA Victor LPM-1515, mono, red vinyl, "DRL" number in trail-
off wax, "BMG Special Products" logo on back cover, from box
"Elvis Top Album Collection Volume 2," 2003.....**10.00 - 20.00**

Mahalo from Elvis

❏ Pickwick ACL-7064, 1978 ....**10.00 - 20.00**

Memories of Christmas

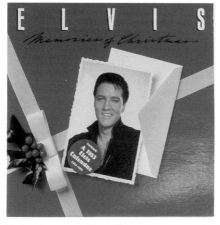

❏ RCA Victor CPL1-4395, with greeting card/calendar
   (deduct 25% if missing), 1982 ....**10.00 - 20.00**

Memories of Elvis
(A Lasting Tribute to the King of Rock 'N' Roll)

❏ RCA Special Products DPL5-0347, five-record set,
   1978...**40.00 - 80.00**

The Memphis Record

❑ RCA 6221-1-R, two-record set, 1987 ....**15.00 - 30.00**

The Million Dollar Quartet

❑ RCA 2023-1-R, with Jerry Lee Lewis, Carl Perkins, and perhaps Johnny Cash, 1990.....................................**12.50 - 25.00**

The Million Dollar Quartet, VOLUME ONE

❑ Sun 1008, with Jerry Lee Lewis, Carl Perkins, and perhaps Johnny Cash, only slicks (never put on an actual cover) exist for this unreleased album, 1977...........................**150.00 - 300.00**

Moody Blue

❑ RCA Victor AFK1-2428, alternate cover slick (never put on an actual cover), with the words "Moody Blue" inside the large word "Elvis"; three copies known to exist; see any late-1970s Elvis inner sleeve for a black and white photo of the scrapped cover, 1977...**2,000 – 3,000**

❑ RCA Victor AFL1-2428, experimental colored vinyl pressings (with no cover); these are known to exist in red, green, white, yellow, gold, purple swirl, and others; price is for any color of vinyl EXCEPT blue or black, 1977.........................**1,000 – 2,000**

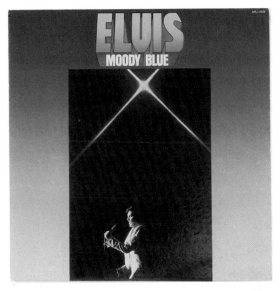

❑ RCA Victor AFL1-2428, black label, dog near top, "Victor" at left; blue vinyl, 1977 .... **5.00 - 10.00**

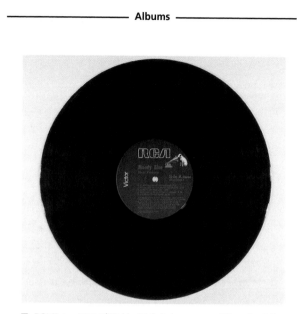

❑ RCA Victor AFL1-2428, black label, dog near top, "Victor" at left; black vinyl, 1977 .... **100.00 - 200.00**

❑ RCA Victor AQL1-2428, black label, dog near top, "Victor" at left; black vinyl, reissue with new prefix, 1979 .... **12.50 - 25.00**

The Number One Hits

❑ RCA 6382-1-R, 1987 .... **15.00 - 30.00**

On Stage February, 1970

❑ RCA Victor LSP-4362, orange label, non-flexible vinyl,
1970..**20.00 - 40.00**

❑ RCA Victor LSP-4362, orange label, flexible vinyl,
1971..**12.50 - 25.00**

❑ RCA Victor LSP-4362, tan label, 1975................**12.50 - 25.00**

❑ RCA Victor LSP-4362, black label, dog near top, "Victor"
at left, 1976..**15.00 - 30.00**

❑ RCA Victor AFL1-4362, Black label, dog near top, "Victor"
at left; includes copies with sticker wrapped around spine
with new number, 1977 ....**6.00 - 12.00**

❑ RCA Victor AQL1-4362, Black label, dog near top, "Victor" at left;
reissue with some cover changes, 1983................**4.00 - 8.00**

The Other Sides: Worldwide 50 Gold Award Hits, Vol. 2

❑ RCA Victor LPM-6402, four-record set, orange labels, flexible
vinyl; with blurb for inserts on cover, 1971.......**35.00 - 70.00**

❑ RCA Victor LPM-6402, 11x33 poster, 1971,
add to above..**12.50 - 25.00**

❑ RCA Victor LPM-6402, swatch of cloth in a white envelope, 1971,
add to above..**12.50 - 25.00**

❑ RCA Victor LPM-6402, four-record set, tan labels, no blurb for
inserts on cover, 1975.....................................**15.00 - 30.00**

❑ RCA Victor LPM-6402, four-record set, black labels,
dog near top, "Victor" at left, 1977 ....**10.00 - 20.00**

Our Memories of Elvis

❑ RCA Victor AQL1-3279, black label, dog near top, "Victor"
at left, 1979 ....**10.00 - 20.00**

Our Memories of Elvis, Volume 2

❑ RCA Victor AQL1-3448, black label, dog near top, "Victor"
at left, 1979 ....**10.00 - 20.00**

Paradise, Hawaiian Style

❑ RCA Victor LPM-3643, mono, "Monaural" on label,
1966 ....**30.00 - 60.00**

❑ RCA Victor LSP-3643, stereo, "Stereo" at bottom of label,
"RCA Victor" at top above dog on black label,
1966 ....**30.00 - 60.00**

❑ RCA Victor LSP-3643, stereo, orange label,
non-flexible vinyl, 1968 ....**20.00 - 40.00**

❑ RCA Victor LSP-3643, stereo, orange label, flexible vinyl,
1971 ....**10.00 - 20.00**

❑ RCA Victor LSP-3643, stereo, tan label, 1975 .... **7.50 - 15.00**

❑ RCA Victor LSP-3643, stereo, black label, dog near top, "Victor" at
left, 1976 ....**6.00 - 12.00**

❑ RCA Victor AFL1-3643, stereo, black label, dog near top, "Victor" at left; includes copies with sticker wrapped around spine with new number, 1977......................................**6.00 - 12.00**

Personally Elvis

❑ Silhouette 10001/2, two-record set, interview records; no music, 1979..**15.00 - 30.00**

The Pickwick Pack (unofficial title)

❑ Pickwick (no #), seven-record set; seven Elvis Pickwick albums in special package and cardboard wrapper; one of the LPs is *Elvis' Christmas Album*, 1978...............................**30.00 - 60.00**

❑ Pickwick (no #), seven-record set; seven Elvis Pickwick albums in special package and cardboard wrapper; one of the LPs is *Frankie and Johnny*, 1979...........................**30.00 - 60.00**

Pot Luck with Elvis

❑ RCA Victor LPM-2523, mono, "Long Play" on label, 1962...**50.00 - 100.00**

❑ RCA Victor LSP-2523, stereo, "Living Stereo" on label, 1962...**75.00 - 150.00**

❑ RCA Victor LPM-2523, mono, "Monaural" on label, 1964...**60.00 - 120.00**

❑ RCA Victor LSP-2523, stereo, "Stereo" at bottom of label, "RCA Victor" at top above dog on black label, 1964....**30.00 - 60.00**

❑ RCA Victor LSP-2523, stereo, orange label, non-flexible vinyl, 1968..**20.00 - 40.00**

❑ RCA Victor LSP-2523, stereo, tan label, 1975.......**10.00 - 20.00**

❑ RCA Victor LSP-2523, stereo, black label, dog near top, "Victor" at left, 1976...**6.00 - 12.00**

❑ RCA Victor AFL1-2523, stereo, black label, dog near top, "Victor" at left; includes copies with sticker wrapped around spine with new number, 1977...**6.00 - 12.00**

Promised Land

❑ RCA Victor APD1-0873, quadraphonic, orange "RCA QuadraDisc" label, "QuadraDisc" on front cover, 1975 ......**100.00 - 200.00**

❑ RCA Victor APL1-0873, stereo, orange label, 1975..**30.00 - 60.00**

❑ RCA Victor APL1-0873, stereo, tan label, 1975 ......**10.00 - 20.00**

❑ RCA Victor AFL1-0873, stereo, black label, dog near top, "Victor" at left, 1977...**7.50 - 15.00**

❑ RCA Victor APD1-0873, quadraphonic, black label, dog near top; "QuadraDisc" on front cover, 1977.................**60.00 - 120.00**

Pure Elvis

❑ RCA Victor DJL1-3455, white label, promo-only item for *Our Memories of Elvis, Volume 2*; contains "unsweetened" versions of four songs on Side 1 and the originally released versions of the same four songs on Side 2, 1979............**300.00 - 600.00**

Pure Gold

❑ RCA Victor ANL1-0971(e), orange label, 1975........ **7.50 - 15.00**

❑ RCA Victor ANL1-0971(e), yellow label, 1976 .... **6.00 - 12.00**

❑ RCA Victor AYL1-3732, yellow label, includes copies with sticker wrapped around spine with new number, 1980......**4.00 - 8.00**

Raised on Rock/For Ol' Times Sake

❑ RCA Victor APL1-0388, orange label, 1973...........**15.00 - 30.00**

❑ RCA Victor APL1-0388, tan label, 1975...............**15.00 - 30.00**

❑ RCA Victor APL1-0388, Black label, dog near top, 1977...**6.00 - 12.00**

Reconsider Baby

❑ RCA Victor AFL1-5418, blue vinyl, 1985...............**12.50 - 25.00**

❑ RCA Victor AFL1-5418, black vinyl, 1985............**10.00 - 20.00**

Remembering

❑ Pair PDL2-1037, two-record set, 1983...............**15.00 - 30.00**

Return of the Rocker

❑ RCA 5600-1-R, 1986 ....**10.00 - 20.00**

Rock 'N Roll Forever

❑ RCA Special Products DML1-0437, 1981 ....**7.50 - 15.00**

Rocker

❏ RCA Victor AFM1-5182, 1984............................**10.00 - 20.00**

Roustabout

❏ RCA Victor LPM-2999, mono, "Mono" on label,
 1964...**50.00 - 100.00**

❏ RCA Victor LSP-2999, stereo, "Stereo" at bottom of label, "RCA
 Victor" in silver above dog on label, 1964......**300.00 - 600.00**

❏ RCA Victor LSP-2999, stereo, "Stereo" at bottom of label, "RCA
 Victor" in white above dog on label, 1964 ....**30.00 - 60.00**

❏ RCA Victor LPM-2999, mono, "Monaural" on label,
 1965...**30.00 - 60.00**

❏ RCA Victor LSP-2999, stereo, orange label, non-flexible
 vinyl, 1968...**20.00 - 40.00**

❏ RCA Victor LSP-2999, stereo, orange label, flexible vinyl,
 1971...**10.00 - 20.00**

❏ RCA Victor LSP-2999, stereo, tan label, 1975........**10.00 - 20.00**

❏ RCA Victor LSP-2999, stereo, black label, dog near top,
 "Victor" at left, 1976 ....**6.00 - 12.00**

❏ RCA Victor AFL1-2999, stereo, black label, dog near top, "Victor"
 at left; includes copies with sticker wrapped around spine with
 new number, 1977.....................................**6.00 - 12.00**

❑ RCA Victor LSP-2999, stereo, red vinyl, "DRL" number in trail-
off wax, "BMG Special Products" logo on back cover, from box
"Elvis Top Album Collection Volume 2," 2003.....**10.00 - 20.00**

2nd to none

❑ RCA 82876-51108-1, 2-record set, 2003 ....**10.00 - 20.00**

Separate Ways

❑ RCA Camden CAS-2611, blue label, 1973 ....**15.00 - 30.00**

❑ Pickwick CAS-2611, black label, 1975 ....**5.00 - 10.00**

❑ Pickwick CAS-2611, black label, gold vinyl,
experimental pressing, not offered for sale to the
public, 1977...**400.00 - 800.00**

Singer Presents Elvis Singing Flaming Star
and Others

❑ RCA Victor PRS-279, sold only at Singer sewing machine dealers;
reissued on RCA Camden 2304, 1968 ....**50.00 - 100.00**

Something for Everybody

❑ RCA Victor LPM-2370, mono, "Long Play" on label;
   back cover advertises RCA Compact 33 single "I Feel So Bad"/
   "Wild in the Country"and Compact 33 Double
   Elvis by Request, 1961 .... **60.00 - 120.00**

❑ RCA Victor LSP-2370, stereo, "Living Stereo" on label; back cover
   advertises RCA Compact 33 single "I Feel So Bad"/
   "Wild in the Country"and Compact 33 Double
   Elvis by Request, 1961 .... **100.00 - 200.00**

❑ RCA Victor LPM-2370, mono, "Mono" on label; back cover advertises RCA Compact 33 single "I Feel So Bad"/ "Wild in the Country"and Compact 33 Double *Elvis by Request*, 1963 .... **40.00 - 80.00**

❑ RCA Victor LSP-2370, stereo, "Stereo" at bottom of label, "RCA Victor" in silver at top of black label; back cover advertises *Elvis' Christmas Album and His Hand in Mine* LPs and Viva Las Vegas EP, 1963 .... **50.00 - 100.00**

❑ RCA Victor LPM-2370, mono, "Monaural" on label; back cover advertises *Elvis' Christmas Album and His Hand in Mine* LPs and Viva Las Vegas EP, 1964 .... **25.00 - 50.00**

❑ RCA Victor LSP-2370, stereo, "Stereo" at bottom of label, "RCA Victor" in white at top of black label; back cover advertises *Elvis' Christmas Album and His Hand in Mine* LPs and Viva Las Vegas EP, 1964 .... **25.00 - 50.00**

❑ RCA Victor LSP-2370, stereo, orange label, non-flexible vinyl; final back cover change advertises *Elvis (NBC-TV Special), How Great Thou Art and His Hand in Mine* LPs, 1968 .... **20.00 - 40.00**

❑ RCA Victor LSP-2370, stereo, orange label, flexible vinyl, 1971 .... **10.00 - 20.00**

❑ RCA Victor LSP-2370, stereo, tan label, 1975 .... **10.00 - 20.00**

❑ RCA Victor LSP-2370, stereo, black label, dog near top, "Victor" at left, 1976 .... **6.00 - 12.00**

❑ RCA Victor AFL1-2370, stereo, black label, dog near top, "Victor" at left; includes copies with sticker wrapped around spine with new number, 1977................................**6.00 - 12.00**

❑ RCA Victor AYL1-4116, stereo, black label, dog near top, "Victor" at lef; includes copies with sticker wrapped around spine with new number, 1981................................**4.00 - 8.00**

❑ RCA Victor LSP-2370, stereo, red vinyl, "DRL 13270" in trail-off wax, "BMG Special Products" logo on back cover, from box "Elvis Top Album Collection Volume 1," 2003.....**10.00 - 20.00**

Special Christmas Programming

❑ RCA Victor UNRM-5697/8, white label, promo only; legitimate copies are 12 inches across and on black vinyl; copies that are 10 inches across and/or on colored vinyl are counterfeits; add 25% for script, 1967................................**600.00 – 1,200**

Special Palm Sunday Programming

❑ RCA Victor SP-33-461, white label, promo only; legitimate copies have trail-off numbers stamped in the wax, while counderfeits have them etched in the wax; add 25% for cue sheet, 1967................................**350.00 - 700.00**

Speedway

❑ RCA Victor LPM-3989, mono, "Monaural" on label, 1968................................**1, 500 – 2,000**

❏ RCA Victor LSP-3989, stereo, "Stereo" at bottom of label, "RCA Victor" in white above dog on black label, 1968 . **30.00 - 60.00**

❏ RCA Victor LPM/LSP-3989, bonus photo with either version, 1968, add to above . . . . **25.00 - 50.00**

❏ RCA Victor LSP-3989, stereo, orange label, non-flexible vinyl, 1968 . . . . **20.00 - 40.00**

❏ RCA Victor LSP-3989, stereo, orange label, flexible vinyl, 1971 . . . . **10.00 - 20.00**

❏ RCA Victor LSP-3989, stereo, tan label, 1975 . . . . . . **10.00 - 20.00**

❏ RCA Victor LSP-3989, stereo, black label, dog near top, "Victor" at left, 1976 . . . . **6.00 - 12.00**

❏ RCA Victor AFL1-3989, stereo, black label, dog near top, "Victor" at left; includes copies with sticker wrapped around spine with new number, 1977 . . . . **6.00 - 12.00**

Spinout

❏ RCA Victor LPM-3702, mono, "Monaural" on label, 1966 . . . . **30.00 - 60.00**

❏ RCA Victor LSP-3702 , stereo, "Stereo" at bottom of label, "RCA Victor" in white above dog on black label, 1966 . **30.00 - 60.00**

❏ RCA Victor LPM/LSP-3702, bonus photo with either version, 1966, add to above . . . . **30.00 - 60.00**

❏ RCA Victor APL1-2560, stereo, black label, dog near top, "Victor" at left, 1977 . . . . **6.00 - 12.00**

❑ RCA Victor AYL1-3684, stereo, black label, dog near top, "Victor" at left, 1980 . . . . **4.00 - 8.00**

The Sun Sessions

❑ RCA Victor APM1-1675, tan label, 1976 . . . . **10.00 - 20.00**

❑ RCA Victor APM1-1675, black label, dog near top, "Victor" at left, 1976 . . . . **6.00 - 12.00**

❑ RCA Victor AFM1-1675, black label, dog near top, "Victor" at left; includes copies with sticker wrapped around spine with new number, 1977 . . . . **7.50 - 15.00**

❑ RCA Victor AYM1-3893, black label, dog near top, "Victor" at left; includes copies with sticker wrapped around spine with new number, 1981 . . . . **4.00 - 8.00**

The Sun Years — Interviews and Memories

❑ Sun 1001, with "Memphis, Tennessee" on label; light yellow cover, brown print, 1977 . . . . **12.50 - 25.00**

❑ Sun 1001, with "Nashville, U.S.A." on label; dark yellow cover with brown print, 1977 . . . . **7.50 - 15.00**

❑ Sun 1001, with "Nashville, U.S.A." on label; white cover with brown print, 1977 . . . . **5.00 - 10.00**

That's the Way It Is

❏ RCA Victor LSP-4445, orange label, non-flexible vinyl,
1970 ....**40.00 - 80.00**

❏ RCA Victor LSP-4445, orange label, flexible vinyl,
1971 ....**12.50 - 25.00**

❏ RCA Victor LSP-4445, tan label, 1975 ....**10.00 - 20.00**

❏ RCA Victor LSP-4445, black label, dog near top,
"Victor" at left, 1976 ....**7.50 - 15.00**

❏ RCA Victor AFL1-4445, black label, dog near top,
"Victor" at left; includes copies with sticker wrapped
around spine with new number, 1977 ....**6.00 - 12.00**

❏ RCA Victor AYL1-4114, black label, dog near top,
"Victor" at left; includes copies with sticker wrapped
around spine with new number, 1981 ....**4.00 - 8.00**

30 #1 Hits

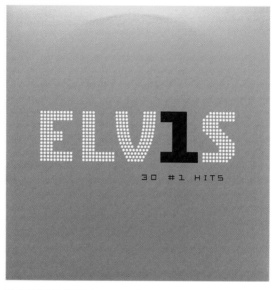

❑ RCA 07863-68079-1, two-record set, 2002 ....**10.00 - 20.00**

This Is Elvis

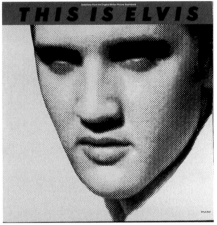

- ❏ RCA Victor CPL2-4031, two-record set, 1980 .... **7.50 - 15.00**

To Elvis: Love Still Burning

- ❏ Fotoplay FSP-1001, picture disc, all tribute songs, in plastic bag with 11x11 insert, 1978 .... **12.50 - 25.00**

- ❏ Fotoplay FSP-1001, picture disc, all tribute songs, in white cardboard cover with black printing, 1978 .... **15.00 - 30.00**

- ❏ Fotoplay FSP-1001, picture disc, all tribute songs, in black cardboard cover with white printing, 1978 .... **7.50 - 15.00**

The Top Ten Hits

❑ RCA 6383-1-R, two-record set, 1987 ....**15.00 - 30.00**

24 Karat Hits!

❑ DCC Compact Classics LPZ-2040, two-record set, numbered
  limited edition, 1997 ....**60.00 - 120.00**

A Valentine Gift for You

❑ RCA Victor AFL1-5353, red vinyl, 1985 ....**10.00 - 20.00**

❑ RCA Victor AFL1-5353, black vinyl, 1985 .... **7.50 - 15.00**

Vintage 1955 Elvis

❑ Oak 1003, 1990 ....**30.00 - 60.00**

Welcome to My World

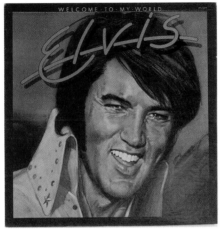

❑ RCA Victor APL1-2274, black label, dog near top, "Victor" at left, 1977...**10.00 - 20.00**

❑ RCA Victor AFL1-2274, black label, dog near top, "Victor" at left; includes copies with sticker wrapped around spine with new number, 1977 ....**6.00 - 12.00**

❑ RCA Victor AQL1-2274, black label, dog near top, "Victor" at left; includes copies with sticker wrapped around spine with new number, 1979 ....**5.00 - 10.00**

Worldwide 50 Gold Award Hits, Vol. 1

❑ RCA Victor LPM-6401, four-record set, orange labels, non-flexible vinyl; with blurb for photo book on cover, 1970 . .**40.00 - 80.00**

❑ RCA Victor LPM-6401, four-record set, orange labels, flexible vinyl; with blurb for photo book on cover, 1970 .**40.00 - 80.00**

❑ RCA Victor LPM-6401, 16-page photo book with either version; two different books exist; the price is for either, 1970, add to above. . . . .**20.00 - 40.00**

❑ RCA Victor LPM-6401, four-record set, tan labels, no blurb for photo book, no book, 1975. . . . .**20.00 - 40.00**

❑ RCA Victor LPM-6401, four-record set, black labels, dog near top, "Victor" at left, 1977 . . . .**15.00 - 30.00**

Worldwide Gold Award Hits, Parts 1 & 2

❑ RCA Victor R 213690, two-record set, RCA Record Club version; one label is orange, the other is tan (orange label on both records is unknown), 1974 . . . .**60.00 - 120.00**

❑ RCA Victor R 213690, two-record set, RCA Record Club version; both labels are tan, 1974. . . . .**20.00 - 40.00**

❑ RCA Victor R 213690, two-record set, RCA Record Club version; black labels, dog near top, "Victor" at left, 1977. .**12.50 - 25.00**

Worldwide Gold Award Hits, Parts 3 & 4

❑ RCA Victor R 214657 [(2)], RCA Record Club version; black
labels, dog near top, "Victor" at left, 1978 ....**10.00 - 20.00**

You'll Never Walk Alone

❑ RCA Camden CALX-2472, blue label, record has "CALX" prefix,
cover has "CAL" prefix, 1971...........................**7.50 - 15.00**

❑ RCA Camden CAL-2472, blue label, both record and cover have
"CAL" prefix, 1974....................................**15.00 - 30.00**

❑ Pickwick CAL-2472, black label, 1975.................**5.00 - 10.00**

It's unlikely we'll ever see another star shine as brightly as Elvis.